"A fascinating, wholly original exploration of d....... ......—a subject with a long history, it appears, of making Americans feel anxious. Along the way, this charming, sprightly yet subversive book probes many a taboo about race and class." —Kennedy Fraser, author of *The Fashionable Mind*

"Original . . . Hats, hems, corsets, collars are all scrutinized in this provocative study." —Barbara Fisher, *The Boston Globe*

"Jenna Weissman Joselit shows how clothes make not just the man or woman but the citizen, indeed the society. Her book is insightful, witty, and bejeweled with detail. If you care as deeply about culture as couture, then this is the book for you." —Samuel G. Freedman, author of *Jew vs. Jew*

"Colorful . . . Joselit dives into a subject many approach but few conquer: She makes sense of fashion." —Linda Gillan Griffin, *Houston Chronicle*

"Most fashion fans just want to know what's hot, what's new, what's next. But for those who like to dig further back in the closet, there's *A Perfect Fit* . . . Engaging." —Linda Crosson, *The Dallas Morning News*

"This sparkling book asks a significant question: How did fashion become a concern not only of socialites but of our grandmothers and great-grandfathers—people whose own parents barely possessed a change of clothes? With marvelous style, she reveals the hidden meanings of hats, shoes, furs, and hemlines, illuminating both our family photographs and our consumer culture, and shows once again the wealth of meaning in the ordinary details of daily life." —Susan Strasser, author of *Waste and Want*

"Joselit, no lightweight, keeps her thesis smart and entertaining, and the pictures are wonderful." —*Flaunt*

"Skillful . . . Ms. Joselit explores the development of fashion as a test of self-restraint and discipline and ultimately, Americanness. . . . I simply didn't want a book this interesting to end." —*The Blade* (Toledo)

"Engaging . . . Joselit succeeds in making readers think about something as familiar as clothing in altogether new ways."
—Sandee Brawarsky, *The Jewish Week*

A Perfect Fit

A Perfect Fit

Clothes, Character, and the Promise of America

JENNA WEISSMAN JOSELIT

A Metropolitan/Owl Book   Henry Holt and Company, New York

Henry Holt and Company, LLC
Publishers since 1866
115 West 18th Street
New York, New York 10011

Henry Holt® is a registered trademark of
Henry Holt and Company, LLC.

Distributed in Canada by H. B. Fenn and Company Ltd.

Library of Congress Cataloging-in-Publication Data
Joselit, Jenna Weissman.
    A perfect fit : clothes, character, and the promise
of America / Jenna Weissman Joselit.
        p.   cm.
    Includes bibliographical references and index.
    ISBN 0-8050-5487-1 (pbk.)
        1. Fashion—Social aspects—United States—
    19th century. 2. Fashion—Social aspects—
    United States—20th century. 3. Clothing and
    dress—United States. I. Title.
TT504.4 .J67 2001
391'.00973'09034—dc21   00-069540

Henry Holt books are available for
special promotions and premiums.
For details contact: Director, Special Markets.

First published in hardcover in 2001 by Metropolitan Books
First Owl Books Edition 2002
A Metropolitan/Owl Book
Designed by Fritz Metsch
Printed in the United States of America
1 2 3 4 5 6 7 8 9 10

To the memory of my grandmother
Rochel Leah Snyder

One-third of your life is spent in bed,
two-thirds of your life in Clothes.

E. L. BRENTLINGER, 1913

Dear Lord, Bless us and help us all to be stylish.

CURRENT LITERATURE, 1902

Contents

A Perfect Fit

Introduction

Once upon a time, Americans placed their faith in clothing. A
snappy suit and a smart hat, they believed, not only buoyed the
spirits but made women pretty and men handsome, promoted
good health and discipline, and built community. Why, with the
right outfit, one could even elude the restraints of class. If you
dressed in a becoming manner, there was absolutely no reason to
be "tabooed," asserted the author of one popular etiquette manual
geared toward the upwardly mobile. "Your clothes are your visiting cards, your cards of admission." No wonder, then, that Americans who came of age between the 1890s, when this book begins,
and the 1930s, when it ends, endowed their clothes with so much
meaning and possibility. Getting dressed was serious business.

The stuff of countless sermons and editorials as well as dreams,
clothing loomed large on the national agenda in the years between

1890 and 1930, a period during which the institutions of modern America—the ballot box and the blaze of electricity, the metropolis and the melting pot—came into their own. In a democracy like ours, explained reformer Ida Tarbell, elaborating on clothing's relationship to the modern polity, how one dressed was not "merely a personal problem" but a national one. Tarbell did not exaggerate. At a time when the challenges of integrating millions of newly emancipated African Americans and newly arrived immigrants weighed heavily on the American body politic, the custodians of American values had much to say about the style, cut, and color of everyday attire. What one wore, they claimed, transforming personal appearance into a civic virtue, was no private affair, subject to fancy or the whim of the moment. What one wore was a public construct, bound up with an enduring moral order. Insisting that America ought to be a nation whose citizens shared the same "national taste in dress," social reformers, schoolteachers, and religious leaders championed the sartorial imperative—and promise—of fitting in. The "question of clothes," they asserted, was a vital "element in the growth of the kind of democracy we need in America," or, as fashion arbiter Mary Brooks Picken put it, in this "great democracy" of ours, the only distinction Americans held dear was that of "appropriateness of dress." In America, there were no social divisions, she ringingly declared. "Here daughters from every country are blended in the making of American women!"

Those on the margins, from the daughters and sons of the foreign-born to the daughters and sons of African American slaves, took careful note of these declarations and set their sights on dressing like everyone else. Better yet, they aspired to dressing like "Mrs. Astorbilt," as the ambitious Sonya Vrunsky, heroine of Anzia Yezierska's immigrant tale *Salome of the Tenements* cleverly puts it, referring, of course, to the worldly Mrs. Astor, the doyenne of high society. For women like Sonya, wearing a stylish ensemble was "in itself culture and education," a way of laying claim to America. Many immigrant men felt the same way. "I was forever watching and striving to imitate the dress and the ways of the well-bred American merchants," recalled one East European immigrant whose entire wardrobe in the Old World consisted of a pair of pants and a few rough-textured shirts. "A whole book could be written on the influence of a starched collar and a necktie on a man who was brought up as I was." Members of the African American community were equally attuned to the opportunities as well as the obligations of dress. A mixed blessing, the wearing of nice clothes "gives to the average woman a confidence and a poise that seems to be a part of her birthright," observed one African American woman. But with that poise and confidence came responsibility for setting a good example, for "bearing the burden of posterity and the burden of the race."

Meanwhile, the triumph of America's ready-to-wear industry and, with it, the growing availability of attractive yet inexpensively produced hats, gloves, blouses, suits, shoes, and even jewelry—much of it produced by immigrant hands—made possible the promise of fitting in. Stylish clothes, once the exclusive preserve of the well-heeled and the well-to-do, were now within everyone's reach. Revolutionizing the way America dressed, ready-to-wear transformed the American woman into the "best-dressed *average* woman in the world" and her menfolk into men-about-town. Advertising, in turn, furthered the public's awareness and acceptance of ready-to-wear by stressing its reliability, probity, and up-to-dateness. Automobile advertisers, in particular, promoted "clothes consciousness" and sparked the public's interest in ready-to-wear, according to A. F. Allison, secretary of the International Association of Garment Manufacturers. Pictures of handsomely attired people admiring an equally handsome, streamlined car inspired a "desire to appear at one's best" and brought home to Americans on "every farm, in every hamlet, town and city, the significance and personal value of the well-dressed look." Etiquette manuals and magazines like *Vogue*, a "fairy godmother" for the fashion-minded, did much the same thing. With a careful, almost mathematical attention to detail and a penchant for charts and tables, these publications not only rationalized the often helter-skelter business of getting dressed but also promoted an inclusive notion of "correctness." To look modern, smart, and appropriate, all anyone had to do was to consult a "guide to correct dress" and follow its strictures.

Taken together, these social and economic forces loosened the hold of social class on the American imagination and gave rise to the "democracy of beauty." Now more attuned to fashion's possibilities than they had ever been before, Americans from all walks of life—farmer's wives and immigrant factory workers, businessmen and boulevardiers—paid increasingly close attention to the clothes on their backs. With eager anticipation, they enrolled in R. H. Macy's Dress-of-the-Month Club, sent away to the Curtis Publishing Company for information on how to obtain a new outfit ("I want pretty clothes too. Will you please tell me how to earn for them"), paid homage to the great Temple of Fashion (or Palace of Fashion, as it was also known) at Philadelphia's Sesquicentennial International Exposition of 1926, and routinely staged fashion shows in which "Mrs. Well Dressed" squared off against "Mrs. Poorly Dressed." On stage and off, fashion was in the air. Transcending class, religion, region, and even race, fashion inspired growing numbers of Americans, men and women alike, to find meaning in the mundane act of getting dressed.

In the pages that follow, I explore the history and cultural consequences of modern America's expanded sartorial awareness. The story that I tell is not the usual one, of Fashion with a capital F and its impact on the *belle monde* and the moneyed. Nor is my story a conventional clothes chronicle or a form of "hemline history." It does not comprehensively chart the ups and downs of women's clothing, take the measure of men's suits, or study the marketplace, the department store, and the factory. Instead, this book explores the relationship between clothes and the character of America, showing how the nation's collective identity was bound up in the warp and woof of its citizens' attire. Today, when fashion is associated with the avant-garde and the cutting edge, with the flouting of convention and the primacy of self-expression, it is hard to imagine a time when fashion had more to do with virtue than with license, with the commonweal rather than the individual. But only a half century ago Americans held fashion to a different standard. Wearing their beliefs on their sleeves, they freighted hats and suits, jewelry and shoes, outerwear and underwear with moral value. Fashion was not simply about looking good. Fashion was about being good as well.

The subject of intense debate—on the street and in the sanctuary, around the dinner table and the water cooler—fashion both registered the most pressing issues of the day and provoked them. In prewar America, the length of a dress, the color of a man's shirt, the size of a hat, the height of a pair of shoes, the sheen of a fur coat, and the glint of a gold bracelet brought to the surface the country's ongoing concern with womanliness and gentlemanliness, religiosity and simplicity, probity and perfectibility even as it focused attention on the health of the nation and the state of its soul. Far from being a mere flourish of history, something altogether incidental to the making of modern America, fashion was the most literal expression of who we were as a nation.

When it comes to the clothes that inhabit this book, much, of course, may strike the contemporary reader as hopelessly old-fashioned. But then, these old things, with their awkward shapes and aspirations, also contain what the late-nineteenth-century historian Alice Morse Earle referred to as the "lingering presence" of the past. "What harmless jealousies, what gentle vanities, what modest hopes linger" in their creases, she noted more than one hundred years ago. Old clothes, she said, "put me truly in touch with the life of my forebears." Like Earle before me, I've come to feel the same way.

The fashion industry was as integral to New York City as the skyscraper.

CHAPTER ONE

À la Mode

"No woman, however hard pressed for time, has a right to look
dowdy nowadays," the *Ladies' Home Journal* categorically declared
in 1925, underscoring the premium America of the twenties placed
on looking "smart" and fashionable. No matter where she lived, in
the city or on a farm, the magazine continued, she could buy stylish, affordable clothes at her local dress shop or department store,
order them from a catalog, or make them herself from pattern
books. The modern American woman could also attend a fashion
show, hear a lecture, and consult all manner of fashion magazines
and guidebooks on the art—and science—of dressing well. With
so many opportunities, she had no excuse for not looking her best
at all times. Like their womenfolk, American men could also avail
themselves of a growing number of sartorial options. No longer
could they blame their wives for their lackluster or even shabby

appearance. ("Men Neglect Clothes to Keep Wives Well-Dressed," proclaimed a headline in the *New York Times,* implying that cost-conscious husbands preferred to adorn their wives rather than themselves.) Now they, too, could purchase a great many things, including colored shirts. "Times have changed," observed the *Saturday Evening Post* in 1931, applauding the way color had emancipated modern man. A glimpse into the wardrobe of the well-dressed man would make the "explorers of Tut-ankh-Amen's tomb green with envy," asserted another student of contemporary mores, referring to the spectacular discovery of the ancient boy king's tomb a decade earlier. "His Royal Highness in Fashion" had nothing on the contemporary American gentleman.

Once the exclusive prerogative of the high and mighty, fashion by the 1920s had become a "social fact" that touched the lives of average people. Calling it one of the "greatest forces in present-day life," Paul Nystrom, a Columbia University professor of marketing, observed in 1928 that fashion had pervaded every field and reached every class. It was fashion that made men shave every day, crease their trousers, and wear shirts with attached collars and that encouraged women to change the "tint of the face powder, the odor of the perfume, the wave of the hair, the position of the waistline, the length of the skirt, the color of the hose, the height of the heels." In short, Nystrom concluded, "to be out of fashion, indeed, is to be out of the world." To be *in* fashion, though, was to be right on top. Offering a new form of identity to millions of Americans across the country, fashion placed within reach an expanded sense of life's possibilities. Women should never underestimate the "psychological effect of clothes," cheered businesswoman Bertha Rich. While a great deal went into making someone a success, the "one asset that *every* woman [could] count on as chief assistant" was her clothes. "First please the eye, and the rest will come easily." Journalist O. O. McIntyre couldn't have agreed more. Clothes not only make the man, he wrote, they "buoy [his] courage."

Mrs. *Goldstein*

Fashionable Dressmaker

119 FORSYTH ST.   NEW YORK

מרם. גאלדשטיין
פעשיאנייבעל דרעססמייקער
119 פארסיט סט.   ניו יארק

Fashion appealed to everyone, including Yiddish-speaking immigrants.

Rich, McIntyre, and increasing numbers of Americans like them associated clothing with pleasure and opportunity. Their parents and grandparents, citizens of the nineteenth century, probably did not. For them, assembling and maintaining a wardrobe was by no means easy. A drain on their finances and their energies, it took some doing. For one thing, those hankering for a stylish new dress or suit had first to purchase the fabric and then find a dressmaker like the chic-sounding Madame DeLyle or a distinguished firm of custom tailors like Howard, Keeler & Scoffield to transform cloth into clothing through the complicated rigamarole of draping, pinning, cutting, and fitting, a process likened to a "cabalistic art." The practice of having one's clothes made also demanded patience and ready cash, both of which were in short supply among everyone but the well-to-do. "I could afford to have only my best dresses made by a regular dress-maker," admitted Anne Aldworth in 1885, adding that her modiste's extravagance in cutting (and wasting) cloth had "long filled me with indignation." Little wonder, then, that most Americans considered a new dress or suit a rarity and stylishness a perquisite of affluence.

The sewing machine simplified the process of making clothes.

Instead, they made do by making their own. Armed with needles, pins, scissors, and thread, thousands of women across America took up sewing. As Aldworth noted, "I cannot help thinking that there must be many others like myself, anxious and ready and willing to do their own simple dress making if only they knew just where and how to make it easy." Aldworth was fortunate: she had her aunt Mary to help her over the rough spots. Sitting at her aunt's side, she watched and took notes as the older woman ran through a series of complicated exercises: "Secure the seam at the waistline first and be very careful not to stretch the cloth . . . then pin about an inch above that, and from there towards the bottom of the waist with the *front* towards you. Now turn it so that the *back* will be towards you and pin from above the waistline towards the top. Baste in the same way." A sensible womanly skill transmitted from one generation to the next, from mother to daughter and from Aunt Mary to her niece Anne, sewing was held in high regard as much for its pedagogic value as for its utility. "Learning to cut, fit and make clothes, pretty clothes," it was widely believed, was critical to the making of a proper young woman. The "practice and art of making clothes which are so far as possible graceful, simple, economical, beautiful should be taught to girls and employed by them in a nation-wide movement if we are to have the best development of our race that our young women are capable of," insisted one fan of this household art, dreaming of an ambitious moral crusade with sewing at its core.

Then again, being clever with the needle was also a vehicle of rectitude, a way of demonstrating the American attributes of thrift and resourcefulness. The "vast army of mothers all over the land" who made their sons' clothing, cheered *Good Housekeeping,* were to be commended for their "practice of economy." The *Ladies' Home Journal,* in turn, approved of those who, dressing themselves as well as their children, knew how to stretch their wardrobes. "To appear well-dressed on a limited income one must be able to sew neatly, must understand how to renovate old materials and have the knack of being able to use and make the most of pieces of old trimming and left-over scraps," advised Emma Hooper, author of the popular monthly column "To Dress Well on a Small Income." A new collar could "brighten up an old bodice as nothing else can," she recommended, while a "circular flounce of broadcloth" did wonders for an otherwise skimpy skirt. Farm women were even more receptive to the art and craft of "clothing renovation," the high-minded name social reformers gave to the process, born of neces-

sity, by which the life of things was extended. Well into the 1910s and 1920s, economically straitened farmers' wives watched and listened carefully as "clothing specialists," home-demonstration agents hired by statewide agricultural extension programs, fanned out across the country teaching them resourcefulness. "Next to poultry, clothing . . . has perhaps the greatest economic and social value of any project in the state," declared agent Agnes Ellen Harris. The program gave the "country

Before the built-in closet, most Americans kept their clothes in wooden wardrobes.

woman self respect and self confidence by making her feel . . . as well dressed as city women." Every year, specialists like Harris and Mary Shaw Gilliam spent thousands of miles on the road, teaching rural woman, especially in the South, how to make, and care for, their clothes. "Good taste in renovation just does not happen," explained Gilliam. "It is ingenuity, plus skill."

Ingenuity, skill, and pedagogy, along with a penchant for language drawn more from the doctor's office than from the sewing room, came together in classes on the making of "children's clothes from leftovers" and at so-called clothes clinics where "worn, cut, 'dejected' garments would be rejuvenated." A South Carolina woman who attended one such clinic recalled that "club members and friends gathered and brought every imaginable kind of clothing and hats. The doctor (agent) and nurses (local leaders) examined these garments and prescribed the necessary treatment." At the end of the day, 337 dresses and 19 hats had been remodeled, 101 boys' suits made from men's old clothing, and 141 slips fashioned from old nightgowns and "thin dresses." Elsewhere in the South, clothing specialists experimented with the "humble flour and food sack," using the sturdy material to create inexpensive and durable clothing for the entire family. The experiment turned out to be a great success, inspiring several Alabama women like Mrs. M. E. Bishop of Talladega County and Mrs. Wilbur Hull of Limestone County to turn chicken-feed bags into an ensemble of dresses and matching hats. These items "would have done credit to a professional modiste," crowed one eyewitness. "Everyone seemed to think they were so pretty."

Despite such encomia, sewing was arduous work. Almost as laborious and time-consuming as fittings at the dressmaker's, the domestic production of clothing required nimble fingers, a good eye, and a sense of proportion, qualities that were often as hard to find as patience. As a result, homemade clothing frequently looked homemade, with a distinctive, sad-sack appearance. Two technological improvements, though—the advent of the domestic sewing

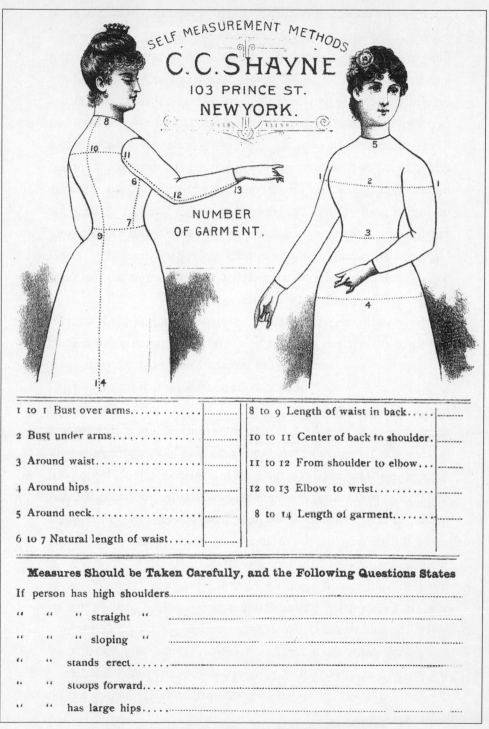

SELF MEASUREMENT METHODS

C.C.SHAYNE
103 PRINCE ST.
NEW YORK.

NUMBER
OF GARMENT.

1 to 1 Bust over arms.............	8 to 9 Length of waist in back.....
2 Bust under arms..............	10 to 11 Center of back to shoulder.
3 Around waist.................	11 to 12 From shoulder to elbow...
4 Around hips.................	12 to 13 Elbow to wrist..........
5 Around neck................	8 to 14 Length of garment........
6 to 7 Natural length of waist......	

Measures Should be Taken Carefully, and the Following Questions States

If person has high shoulders..

"   "   " straight   " ....

"   "   " sloping   " ....

"   " stands erect...... ....

"   " stoops forward.... ....

"   " has large hips.... ....

Making a dress or a blouse required a good sense of human anatomy.

machine and the mass production and dissemination of inexpensive paper dress patterns—not only made sewing easier, "as if done by fairy fingers," but also professionalized the final product, rendering it more attractive. By the 1870s, women everywhere could be found carefully spreading tissue-thin dress patterns on their kitchen tables or parlor floors and tracing the outlines of a bodice or a sleeve onto a bolt of fabric, following the helpful directions that companies like E. Butterick & Company made a point of providing. (Sometimes, however, instructions were so complicated that "none but students of higher mathematics could possibly master" them.) Placing the fabric in the sewing machine, the home sewer would effortlessly baste and seam until, with a real show of "yankee ingenuity," a reasonably well-fitting, somewhat stylish garment emerged from her labors—all for under a few dollars.

Even with these latter-day improvements, not all women acquitted themselves well. At first, everything went according to plan, recalled one woman of her initial efforts at using a paper pattern to make a "waist," or blouse. "The directions were easy to follow and I succeeded in saving a great deal of cloth." But when it came time to try on the garment, it "wrinkled here and there in a strange way that puzzled me. I took it off and looked at it, but could discover nothing wrong; again I put it on and took it off in despair, and finally after taking in a seam here and letting out one there, and pulling and smoothing all to no effect, I became disgusted and threw the waist across the room and shed bitter, bitter tears." Some women clearly lacked the requisite skills, or else they found sewing much too tedious. Women wrote to say they didn't know how to sew, an exasperated Emma Hooper noted. They would have to learn, she told them. Other women wrote to say they loved to sew but sewing made them nervous. To them, Hooper suggested "they try to sew when tired and to rest every fifteen or twenty minutes."

Such sage advice, for all its good intentions, frequently fell on deaf ears. Many American women, lacking either the manual or the mental dexterity required to sew, relied instead on their elders or on the kindness of strangers to obtain their clothes. In households across America, clothing led many lives: a pair of pants worn by Johnny one year was invariably handed down to younger brother Jimmy the next, and a dress worn by Margaret was passed on to her baby sister Molly. The practice of hand-me-downs was as regular as the seasons and just as essential. Critical to the household economy, hand-me-downs could either be worn as they had been or taken apart and reassembled to make something new. Writing in *Good Housekeeping* in 1885, Helen N. Packard urged modern mothers to take the time and trouble to make "little knee pants" for their young sons from the jackets and trousers discarded by the older men of the house: "It certainly requires no more patience or brains than crazy patchwork and is far more useful."

Meanwhile, those favored mortals blessed with affluence and able to outfit themselves as well as their sons and daughters in new rather than renovated clothing were encouraged to donate their discards to charity. The lady of the house should see to it that outworn clothing did not "become food for . . . moths," advised the bible of sanitary science. "But rather she will cast her mind around to see on whom she can bestow" these items, "where they will be sure to be utilized." There would be people somewhere who would have their "hearts gladdened and their bodies made warm and neat at slight expense and trouble." Taking such suggestions to heart, church and synagogue sisterhoods as well as women's associations like the New-York Clothing Society for the Relief of the Industrious Poor and the Hebrew Ladies Sewing Society of Alabama made sure to help those in need. Members, "busy in the interest of others," got together several afternoons a week to make clothes for those less fortunate, a task as enjoyable as it was necessary. One devotee was so proud of her group's output that she likened her temple's sewing room to a commercial establishment. When not sewing, women's groups collected items they or their kinfolk had either outgrown or tired of wearing and, through "gift chests," rummage sales, and bazaars, saw to their distribution. In each instance, clothing was the currency of women's philanthropy.

Women's organizations also tried their hand at running thrift shops where, it was hoped, consumers would not feel like second-class citizens for having purchased something secondhand. In an atmosphere redolent of a "little" ladies dress shop, the thrift shop married the principles of merchandising with charity, treating those in need as customers rather than as supplicants. Every item received was carefully inspected, sensibly priced, and attractively displayed. Along the way, the thrift shop succeeded in generating a good deal of income for its charitable sponsors. What better incentive than charity, after all, to get women to rummage through the family attic in search of something to give away? The thrift shop also succeeded in professionalizing women's skills. "After an apprenticeship in thrift-shop merchandising, even a novice becomes as confident as any careerist," declared a representative of the Council of Jewish Women, noting how the Council Shop encouraged women to draw on their "latent flair for advertising." Ultimately, the thrift shop was more than just a morally uplifting form of housekeeping or a big moneymaker, one of its fans explained. "It means dignity and self-respect for many families. . . . They pay for what they get and they select what they please." Besides, she added, "it's a lot of fun."

The secondhand clothing store went even further than the thrift shop in its commercializing of hand-me-downs and castoffs. An outright business venture, traffic in used clothing flourished in metropolitan America. With the cry "I buy! I cash clothes!" ringing through the streets, the presence of the "ole-clo's man" was familiar to generations of urban American housewives. Carrying

Filled with goods, charitably run thrift shops were managed by women.

May future, with her kindest smile,
Wreath Laurels for thy brow;
May loving angels guard and keep thee
Ever pure as thou art now.

JOSEPH M. COHEN,
Highest Cash price paid for Cast-off
CLOTHING.
CALL OR ADDRESS'
No, 1547 Callowhill Street,
PHILADELPHIA,

Daintily illustrated trade cards took the sting out of castoffs.

brown wrapping paper for his purchases and a tightly folded newspaper ("This is the sign I buy, he says"), the old-clothes peddler canvassed the city for hours on end in search of discarded clothing, purchasing a pair of shoes for a quarter and a suit for a dollar. "I like to walk," said one peddler, explaining why he took up the trade in the first place. "I like the fresh air." By the end of the day, piles of used clothing would find a temporary resting place atop the dusty, cramped shelves of a secondhand retail clothing store. For years, the stock-in-trade of the secondhand store consisted almost entirely of men's furnishings and its clientele of men in straitened circumstances. "Fully 50% of men's clothing finds it way into the secondhand stores or is offered for sale on the streets," observed *Harper's Weekly* in 1911, devoting a full page to a colorful description of New York's secondhand clothing trade, where "one buys and sells without fear and without reproach." Downtown, at the site of the "greatest secondhand clothing business in the New or in the Old World"—or, for that matter, in the other urban immigrant enclaves that clothing dealers called home—male customers could purchase a pair of trousers ("always known as 'pants' in that locality") for fifteen cents, an overcoat for twenty. Women's apparel, in contrast, comprised a small fraction of the secondhand clothing store's stock, at least before the advent of ready-to-wear. The gentler sex, it seemed, had a "knack for remaking and remodeling their garments so many times that, when at last . . . their days of usefulness have passed, they are then fit only for the bag of the rag-picker."

There were some exceptions: women who sold their things and women who bought them. In the wake of the First World War, it became common practice, especially among society women, to sell their cast-off clothing, explained Aaron Kosofsky, reportedly the largest secondhand dealer in the world, with estimated revenues of $3 million a year. The "rich society leader," having worn an expensive gown two or three times, tired of it and sold it to someone like him, sending "Fifi, the French maid, or James, the butler, to do the bargaining. Usually, the butler and the maid drive better bargains than Madame would drive herself." Customers included shopgirls and stenographers, "business girls," aspiring actresses, teachers, and the wives of underpaid postmen, firemen, and other civil service employees. For $12 or $15 they could purchase a gown or a frock that originally cost anywhere from $125 to $200; typically, it was not only in mint condition but in the very latest style, to boot.

Even so, delight at finding a wonderfully priced and fashionable, if slightly worn, dress or suit went only so far. Often, it carried a steep emotional price. "It is no light achievement, the living up to and into other people's clothes," recalled one man. "Clothes acquire so much personality from their first wearer—they adjust themselves to the swell of the chest, the quirk of the elbow, the hitch in the hip joint—that the first wearer always wears them." The first wearer left a permanent imprint in other ways as well, making subsequent wearers feel as if they inhabited someone's else soul or, worse still, had none to call their own. As Fanny Brice poignantly put it in her signature song:

It's no wonder that I feel abused,
I never have a thing that ain't been used.
I'm wearing second hand hats, second hand clothes,
That's why they call me Second Hand Rose.

Enormously popular, the song evoked a world that associated used clothing with deprivation. But that would soon change. Thanks to the growing availability of ready-to-wear, sentiments like those voiced by Second Hand Rose were becoming less and less common and the strategies that gave rise to them less and less necessary. Fewer and fewer people whiled away the hours at the dressmaker's or the tailor's; as a result, such establishments, once ubiquitous, were in decreasing demand. Sewing, too, suffered an irreversible decline in popularity. To be sure, modern American women did not completely forsake the sewing machine for the clothes rack. Some continued to find a "deep sense of satisfaction" and "lasting contentment" in making their own clothes. Others thrilled to the prospect of saving money, of dressing "better for less." When you made your own clothes, related one enthusiast, you had more "dollars in your purse." True enough. Even more undeniable, though, was the marked change in sewing's status: once a necessity, it was fast becoming an optional pursuit. Ready-to-wear had taken its place.

Said to employ more people than the sprawling steel mills of Pittsburgh, the motorcar plants of Detroit, or the slaughterhouses of Chicago, the ready-to-wear industry, headquartered in New York City, altered America's access to and attitude toward dress. For one thing, mass-produced clothing now speedily made its way from one end of the country to the other. An intricate network of manufacturers, jobbers, and buyers, catering to a wide range of consumers, from those able to "indulge a fat purse" to those who "coddled a lean one," ensured that an "Easter parade model" fabricated in New York would easily "fit into the picture of almost any American city." Typically, a dress or a suit would travel from

SINGER SEWING LIBRARY—No. 1

SHORT CUTS
TO
HOME SEWING

The Modern Singer Way

PUBLISHED BY
SINGER SEWING MACHINE CO. INC.

In modern America, sewing increasingly became more of a hobby than a necessity.

a fancy atelier on Fifth Avenue to Fourteenth Street, where a manufacturer of midpriced garments would produce a copy. A week or so later, a low-priced house on, say, Grand and Canal would come up with an even more inexpensive version, and so on down the chain, until the dress found itself on the racks of five-and-dimes throughout the country. Why, even farm girls, observed the *New York Times* in 1926, could have pretty clothes.

By that point, a dazzling array of affordable fashions beckoned from coast to coast, from department stores in midtown Manhattan to little ladies' shops in Niles, California, affording Mr. and Mrs. Consumer a great deal of latitude. Stern Brothers bragged of "distinctive new apparel authentically correct for every hour of the day," while its rival, B. Altman & Company, insisted that "clothes for men, clothes for women, for misses and for the younger set"—in fact, "everything that is new and smart in clothes for every occasion"—could be obtained at its Fifth Avenue emporium. In Los Angeles, Bullock's went a step further by classifying its wares in terms not of gender, age, or novelty but of personality, six different versions' worth, including the "romantic" ("rose-wreathed hats"), the "statuesque" ("trailing negligees"), the "artistic" ("eccentric jewelry" and berets), the "picturesque" ("soft, unassertive fabrics"), the "modern" ("boyish and sleek"), and the "conventional" ("economical dress"). As Bullock's made abundantly clear, in the world of ready-mades there was something for everyone: "adorable" bathing suits, "slenderizing fashions for stout women," sexy prom dresses, "blythe apparel for the leisure class," and jaunty chapeaux.

Even casual housedresses now hung on the racks of the nation's department stores and lingerie shops, thanks to Nell Donnelly of Kansas City. Unable to find "something bright, colorful and cheerful" to wear while working around the house, Mrs. Donnelly resolved to make her own. In no time at all, her designs won raves. "The gay, becoming house dresses . . . were the marvel of the neighborhood," she proudly recalled. Encouraged by her success, Donnelly showed her designs to a local department store buyer, and the rest was history. She and her husband went into business for themselves. Though their company "lacked a Fifth Avenue address," it prospered, soon becoming a leading manufacturer. "The fact that we are able, with all of these prosaic machines, to help make thousands of homes more cheerful and thousands of women prettier at their housework . . . is like a fairy tale come true," Donnelly told a reporter. "No housewife in America today need look dowdy and frumpy, unless she wants to be that way."

Appealing to the imagination and the senses, ready-made clothing reflected modern America. Practical, "serviceable clothing for life in the open" like Kamp-it garments allowed nature lovers to enjoy the great outdoors in comfort while Abercrombie & Fitch's "Lenox ulster" spoke to the "automobilist" of both sexes. Cut on "mannish lines," this coat enhanced the pleasures of driving a car, of "annihilating space and of going at full speed—thirty miles an hour—in accordance with one's fancy and caprice." Working women, in turn, looked "very alert [and] business-like" when outfitted in "honest, efficient clothes free from frills and furbelows," even as their male supervisors looked awfully "spruce" in their suits. And for a night on the town, faithful copies of the swank evening clothes worn by Hollywood stars were increasingly available at popular prices at the Style Shop in Kalamazoo, Michigan, or at the Cinema Shop at Macy's, as were numerous versions of the Little Black Dress, an item that "made so many women look impeccable, if somewhat alike."

With mass-produced creations like these, American fashion, increasingly independent of Paris, the citadel of couture and high style, transformed the nation. No matter how chic a middle-aged, middle-income Parisienne might be, she would never know the "purely American pleasure of walking to a shop in one dress and walking out in another," rhapsodized the *New Yorker*. Immigrants,

Camping clothes promised "absolute protection" from Mother Nature.

for their part, delighted in the magic of ready-to-wear: "Cinderella clothes," one Jewish immigrant writer called them. Though much of America—its rhythms, language, and customs—may have eluded these newcomers, the act of putting on a ready-made suit or shirtwaist made them feel more at home, at least initially. On the outside, immigrants looked American even if, on the inside, they weren't, not quite yet. Newcomer Sophie Abrams, for instance, recalled standing before a mirror, outfitted in a new shirtwaist, skirt, and hat ("such a hat I had never seen"), and saying to her new self, "Boy, Sophie, look at you now . . . just like an American." Rose Gallup felt much the same way about her store-bought clothes, especially her very first purchase, a navy blue cashmere dress, the "first dress I ever had that was not home-made and too large for me." Rose's new acquisition lifted her spirits. "It cost me a week's wages and many tears," she recalled. "But it was worth it. It was so pretty and gave me a great deal of joy." For Rose, Sophie, and countless immigrant women like them, ready-to-wear was not only a source of personal pleasure; ready-to-wear symbolized America—its abundance and flexibility, its choices and resources. Ready-to-wear, proclaimed *Vogue,* aptly capturing its essence, was "as American as turning on—and having—hot-water."

The growing popularity of the fashion show in America of the interwar years underscored fashion's expanded appeal. Manufacturers and department stores, women's auxiliaries and church groups, even 4-H clubs, found its artful blend of consumerism and theatricality hard to resist. In the South, the "mock fashion show" or "economy show," as its creators humorously dubbed it, was a staple of the farm circuit; likewise, in Muncie (aka Middletown), Indiana, "style shows" drew just about everyone in town. "Ten-cent store clerks, tired-looking mothers with children, husbands and wives watched rouged clerks promenade languorously along the tops of the show cases, displaying the latest hats, furs, dresses, shoes, parasols, bags and other accessories, while a jazz orchestra kept everybody 'feeling good.' " Women's groups like the O. Clay Maxwell Club of Harlem's Mount Olivet Baptist Church and Hadassah, the preeminent Zionist women's organization, also claimed the fashion show as their own. Before long, no annual luncheon or convention was complete without some kind of "eye-filling" fashion parade at which amateur models, dressed to the nines, glided down church aisles or stepped out of papier-mâché gardens. Menswear manufacturers also favored shows. Routinely

Fashion shows added a touch of glamour to daily life.

staged at conventions of tailors and other style makers, these productions tended to represent the well-to-do-man in his "natural" setting: at work, on the links, at the opera, or on the bridle path.

Some fashion shows, especially those staged several times a year by the manufacturers of exclusive fashions, were elaborate affairs, veritable panoramas of damask, gilt, and bright lights. As a trio of chamber musicians played softly in the background, one eyewitness related, a group of lithe models took their places on the runway: "And the show is on. Number after number, scene upon scene, follows in breath-taking succession," one creation more "dazzling, brilliant, daring and gorgeous" than the next. From time to time, the production itself, like the second annual Fur Fashion Show of 1922, upstaged the clothes. Devoted to the theme of Winter, the proceedings, held at New York's Hotel Astor, began with a spectacular ballet of "snow babies," followed by youthful pages in Eskimo garb. Emerging from their specially designed snow huts, they heralded the arrival of one fur coat after another as it appeared on the winterized runway. Other fashion shows, like those produced by rural farm women, were, admittedly, far more humble, though no less well received: a bare stage—usually in a high school auditorium—a few props, and homegrown models.

Trickling down from one end of the social scale to the other, the fashion show ranged widely in sensibility, too. While those characteristic of the industry were hushed, serious affairs (after all, a lot of money was at stake), the "fashion promenades" put on by women's philanthropic groups tended more toward "pink mink" and other fanciful inventions. In 1937, for instance, the Wilkes-Barre section of the Council of Jewish Women came up with a novel fashion show in which its members not only acted as mannequins but wore their own fall clothes. Though it sounded simple, this actually took some doing: all of the participants had to promise not to wear their new purchases before the premiere. Less demanding by far was the "Castaway Calvalcade" mounted by the council's Denver branch, which featured local women wearing an array of fashions that spanned their grandmothers' era on through their own. Now *this*, commented one observer, was truly an "unusual fashion show." What a way to teach history! Equally unusual were used-clothing revues. One Los Angeles women's group presented a show in which twenty-five models clad in discarded clothing paraded before an audience of well-heeled women. These models, reported a spectator, certainly looked "smart enough to make [everyone present] want to 'house-clean' [their] old coats, suits and dresses and give them to the Thrift Shop." Meanwhile, in Shelby County, Alabama, thirty women took part in a "dress revue," wearing clothes made entirely out of feed bags. There was "no trace of the big letters that had been a part of every feed sack," reported one local newspaperman, adding, "no one present would have suggested that the ladies were not well dressed."

In fact, the fashion shows produced by rural women and their daughters were extremely inventive, making up in drama what they lacked in spectacle. At a time when riding in trains and cars was an occasion, one Alabama group staged a mock "travelling costume contest," seeking to ascertain who looked better, the "girls who come by train" or the "girls who come in cars."

In the first scene, two women, Katherine and Mary, take their places on the train, whereupon Katherine asks Mary: "Do you think that I am appropriately dressed to travel on the train?"

Mary: "Yes. . . . Your dress looks neat; it is well pressed and clean; it is of simple design, simple color scheme and it is not over-decorated. . . . Yes, I think you are well-dressed."

Katherine: "Well you certainly picked me to pieces but I am glad you approve of me."

In the next scene, Mary espies a group of women in a car; they're wearing any old thing. Pointing to their clothing, she says disapprovingly: "So many people think you can wear just about anything when you come in cars, and I think that you should be just as well-dressed while driving through the country as when travelling on a train. You have to stop in towns for lunch or cold drinks when you are driving. People stop and look at you and the license on your car and wonder what part of the country you come from, if you are not appropriately dressed."

As the curtain comes down, both women agree that there

should be no difference in dress between those who drive a car and those who take the train.

On the runway, good posture was as prized as good looks.

While some fashion shows took place in familiar surroundings, the women of rural Henry County, Alabama, set theirs far away, in the Parisian studio of the renowned couturier Paul Poiret, then at the height of his fame and influence—even in the Deep South. Farm audiences watched raptly as this most "picturesque" of designers offered "some Do's and Don'ts of Fashion for all types of ladies." Women with large busts should avoid wearing curved or V-shaped lines, an actor playing Poiret advised. Instead, they should wear "loose folds which conceal the bust." Large hips called for "lines that go up and down" rather than "lines that go around."

Home economists were equally didactic in their use of the fashion show, hoping to transform high school students into surefooted consumers by teaching them "buymanship." "Teachers are everywhere presenting the subject in new and interesting ways," Zella E. Bigelow observed in 1920, calling on her fellow home economists to put on fashion shows with "living models" and live music to illustrate the challenges confronting the modern consumer. "Posture and walk should be emphasized and all details, such as what to do with the hands, should be taken care of so that nothing will detract from the desired effect"—to train potential consumers to think sagely about the selection and purchase of their wardrobes. Meanwhile, the "clothing contest" was all the rage in Texas and Louisiana, Nevada and North Dakota, where high school students and 4-H club members paraded before panels of domestic scientists to decide whose dress was the most economical and sensible. Such events, according to Lillian Peek of the Texas State Board for Vocational Training, one of its ardent champions, not only developed a spirit of good sportsmanship among the contestants but helped promote simpler ways of dressing and a "wholesome" approach to the "clothing problem." In both instances, fashion was relegated to the background. Instead of emphasizing stylishness, the usual bill of fare at most fashion shows, the didactic fashion show and clothing contest emphasized "suitability, durability, economy, becomingness, health and efficiency." Home economists, eager to rationalize what they considered to be the dangerously subjective processes of evaluation and consumption, even went so far as to publish, and through the good graces of the U.S. Department of Agriculture to circulate, a series of detailed score cards to be used at these kinds of events. A garment's "general appearance" garnered thirty points, "health aspects" were good for ten, "suitability" and "economic factors" such as the cost of upkeep each rated twenty, and "ethics," an elastic rubric that encompassed modesty as well as "social influence," counted for another ten.

Scored or choreographed, the fashion show took hold throughout the nation in the interwar years, becoming a vital part of American culture. Its popularity did more than reflect a fresh and positive attitude toward the pursuit of stylishness. It revealed a democratic understanding of fashion as well.

Not everyone, though, applauded America's sartorial revolution. A broad swath of Americans, from self-styled aesthetes to certified domestic scientists, took to worrying about the social and moral consequences of a nation now at liberty to change its clothes—and its image—at will. Suddenly, fashion became one of the "great topics of the hour." To be sure, the demonization of Dame Fashion was nothing new. Throughout their history, Americans had been warned of her tyrannical ways. "A president can be deposed, an autocrat can be assassinated but against the tyrant Fashion neither votes nor bombs are weapons," thundered the *Independent,* a popular monthly in pre–World War I America, underscoring Dame Fashion's implacability. Some early-twentieth-century Americans, likening her hold on the popular imagination to an addiction, as "fatal a habit as opium or gambling," even went so far as to call for a "new Temperance Union" that would "strive to overcome not only King Alcohol but Dame Fashion." The triumph of ready-to-wear only made matters worse, threatening to ensnare the average citizen—not just the well-heeled—in her web. Reviving talk of fashion's deleteriousness, pundits predicted that no good could ever come from buying off the rack.

The mildest among them objected to mass-produced clothing on aesthetic grounds, lamenting its "hurried" workmanship. Ready-made clothes, declared the *Craftsman,* a leading journal of the American arts and crafts movement, were "ungraceful, foolish and shoddy." Emily Post, the nation's authority on good taste and manners, was among those who turned up their noses at the thought of wearing a mass-produced garment. Awkward and ungainly, ready-to-wear clothes, she wrote dismissively, were "ninety percent freak." They were certainly "no works of art," agreed Florence B. Rose, whose monthly column, "Woman's Realm," held forth on the vagaries of the fashion world. Promoting uniformity at the expense of individuality, ready-mades, said its critics, ignored the varied proportions of the human body in favor of a mannequin's doll-like dimensions and threatened to lower the nation's self-respect in the process. "Women almost universally have a horror of whatever smacks of a uniform," Rose explained. Worse still, ready-mades did not fit nearly as well as a dressmaker's designs, leaving lots of unhappy customers in the dressing room. One department store employee recalled how she inadvertently insulted large-size customers accustomed to the subtle promptings of their dressmaker by suggesting they try the "stylish stout" department. Retailers also added their voice to the chorus of critics. "Sizes askew on women's clothing," the members of the Indiana Retail Dry Goods Association charged in 1926, indicting manufacturers for their failure to take into account the "contours" of the contemporary female customer: Women spent much of their time riding in automobiles and not enough time exercising, but the manufacturers paid no heed to the resulting changes in their figures, alleged the retailers. Mindful only of the proportions of their mannequins rather than those of real women, they had "fallen down on the job," producing ill-fitting clothes that discomfited and disappointed the consumer, whether she was svelte or stylishly stout.

Others within the anti–ready-to-wear camp worried more about disease than discomfort, especially when it came to the possibility of germs nesting in the tucks of a shirtwaist or in the hem of a skirt. Labeling mass-produced clothes as "disease-breeding garments made in unclean and unsafe shops," the health-conscious members of consumer leagues and antituberculosis societies at first urged consumers to play it safe either by making their own or by continuing to patronize dressmakers. Later they joined with the International Ladies' Garment Workers' Union and other labor unions to lobby for improved sanitary conditions in the workplace. Those shops that conformed to higher hygienic standards were encouraged to sew a white label onto their products. The equivalent of a clean bill of health, the white, or sanitary, label sought to reassure anxious consumers that the garment they were about to purchase was germ-free.

More damning than microbes, though, was the danger that

ready-to-wear reportedly posed to the moral health of America's women. "Disaster seems to strike when women seek to dress as stylishly as those they see about them in the shops or on the streets," critics charged, hinting darkly at the possibility of an epidemic of jealousy among those freshly "inoculated with the virus of style." Ready-to-wear, its detractors insisted, took advantage of the female consumer, especially her perennial concern over being in—or out of—style, and made her a slave to fashion. "Crops may fail, silk-worms suffer blight, weavers may strike, tariffs may hamper, but the mass-gesture of the feminine neck bending to the yoke of each new season's fashion goes on," exploded writer Fannie Hurst, insisting on women's utter helplessness in the face of greedy garment manufacturers. Beholden to the "god of novelty," these makers of blouses and dresses deliberately saw to it "that last year's wardrobe shall annually be made as obsolete as possible," thus inflating the fiscal and emotional costs of keeping up appearances. Quite a few women agreed with the critics. More ladies of "good education, interesting surroundings and unusual opportunities" were throwing away their lives in a futile attempt to keep up, related one of their number, bristling at the very idea. "Our minds . . . are prone to be centuries behind the fashion," Mrs. Ernest Jaros of Columbus, Ohio, a stalwart member of the National Council of Jewish Women, glumly concurred, wondering why women paid so much less attention to "mental fashion" than they did to matters of dress. But then, if contemporary wisdom was to be believed, women—rich or poor, black or white, descendants of the *Mayflower* or just off the boat—couldn't help themselves. The genus of woman was categorically unable to resist the seductive accessibility of ready-to-wear, responding to changes in fashion as "automatically as an instantaneous water-heater." The male of the species, fortunately, had no such problem. "Turning styles for men off and on has not been done. It is sometimes attempted, but there seems to be an individuality in fashions for men that defies the regularizing hand."

As ready-to-wear came into its own, giving rise to dozens of handbooks on how to dress, another attitude toward fashion began to emerge, one that harnessed the power of Dame Fashion to the social good. Fashion was not necessarily bad for you, insisted Caroline King Duer, author of *How to Tell the Fashions from the Follies*. On the contrary. If you learned to dress correctly, to distinguish between what was appropriate and what was not, your clothes could give you a good name, not a black eye. Offering up a redemptive rather than a sinful view of fashion, Duer and other champions of ready-to-wear allied clothing with morality and the act of getting dressed with the exercise of virtue. In their eyes, fashion was no longer the mark of excess and inconstancy; instead, it was now bound up with virtuousness and steadfastness—if only consumers followed their advice. Widely available in women's magazines and how-to books, it consisted of the following suggestions:

- Never mind that most folks are wearing ultrastylish articles of wearing apparel. Make it your own business to dress in a way that reveals the "real self that is you."
- "To be fashionable does not mean that you should adopt every new fad just as it is given out; rather, it means that you should intelligently readjust the prevailing style so that it will conform to the lines of your face and your figure."
- Never turn to a "motion-picture personality" for advice or try to copy her style of dressing. "A star's life is hectic and varied. She enjoys the privilege of an actress—to be amusing and slightly sensational." Not so the rest of us. Our days are "keyed to a certain monotony" in which drama is out of place.

Guidebooks to correct dress, dozens of which now lined book-sellers' shelves, were particularly useful for those cursed with a "slim purse and luxurious tastes." It was terrible to "see the world full of decorative ladies in beautiful clothes, [and] not to be able to rush out and imitate them," acknowledged *Vogue*, gallantly rushing to the rescue with the creation of a "Department of Smart Fashions for Limited Incomes." It, too, now jumped on the bandwagon, helping ordinary Americans do right by their clothes. Twice a year, its sketches and observations guided the impecunious on ways to update their wardrobes "so cleverly that nobody but yourself and your cheque-book will know." (The virtues of bows, collars, and cuffs were touted often and exuberantly.) In promoting these features, *Vogue* and its sister experts usually had the "alert, efficient, responsible business girl" in mind. "It is getting harder and harder to sell the cleverest girl to an executive unless she looks and acts like Park Avenue," explained Frances Maule, author of a 1930s tract on success and the working woman. "Your watchword in selecting your office wardrobe should be conservative good taste. . . . Hold fast to the tried and true." Simple but feminine, well-fitting but not too revealing outfits were the ideal; masculine clothes were to be avoided at all cost. ("Men hate them. They give the impression that a woman is competing with him on his own ground instead of supplementing his masculine abilities with her distinctly feminine gifts.") Finally, when it came to jewelry, pearls and a wristwatch were fine. "But no clacking clusters of bracelets or bangles. If you must wear earrings—and it would really be better if you didn't—keep to the simple and not-too-large ear studs."

Gently worded exhortations like these were intended for those women safely ensconced in the middle class or, like Frances Maule's business girl, well on their way. But for the "circumstantially denied," a delicate euphemism for those on the fringes of society like immigrant and African American women, much more needed to be said. After all, the stakes were higher: the right clothing, like the right citizenship papers, conferred acceptability; the wrong clothes provoked disdain, even ostracism. Is it any wonder, then, that the moral custodians within both the Jewish immigrant and the African American communities loudly inveighed against

Immigrant women found America's bounty hard to resist.

Dame Fashion? "The woman who worships at the shrine of fashion loses her bearings," cautioned Fannie Barrier Williams of the National Association of Colored Women's Clubs. "She has no time to read good books, no time to cultivate those things that minister to the refinement and beauty of her home and no time or inclination to contribute her heart and her talents to the social uplift of those about her." Amen to that, responded Rabbi Maurice Harris, who was so disturbed by what he saw in the pews of his congregation and on the streets of his Manhattan neighborhood that he devoted his High Holiday sermon one year to an attack on fashion. The paint, powder, and excessively stylish attire of many Jewish women, charged this latter-day Jeremiah, "awakens the most revolting sensations, and shatters all claims to decency." As a community whose members prided themselves on their collective moral code, he said, American Jews ought to do better.

Living up to high standards was further complicated by the pressures of acculturation. The Jewish immigrant woman was so eager to become an American that she laid "great stress" on clothes, explained Viola Paradise of Chicago's Immigrants' Protective League. After only a few weeks in this country, the newcomer was "convinced" that the "essential thing in America was to 'look stylish.'" Misapprehending the spirit of America, the young Jewish woman then compounded the problem by making mistakes in her choice of attire, selecting that which was "extreme and ugly" over that which was discreet and unobtrusive. She didn't know any better. Young African American women, also exposed to new freedoms, reportedly suffered the same predicament; they, too, it was said, had trouble distinguishing sartorial right from wrong. Given to dressing in bright, gay colors and to wearing satin and silk to church, they were apt to be "conspicuous" rather than quiet. Lamentable as this might be, observed Jane Addams, the legendary social reformer, it made sense. Those at the bottom of society attempted to emulate those well above them, but without much success.

African American women delighted in dressing for church.

"They imitate, sometimes in more showy and often in more trying colors, in cheap and flimsy materials, in poor shoes and flippant hats, the extreme fashions of the well-to-do." In a word: they missed.

Worse still, both groups were believed to be easily led astray by their appetites. A hankering for beautiful clothes, observed Paradise, often culminated in the ruination of an immigrant girl. Realizing that she would never be able to afford as many nice clothes as she wanted, she was "in danger of taking a wrong way to get the luxuries which America has taught her to crave." Williams felt the same. The "fine dressing" displayed on Chicago's State Street on Sunday—a splendid "procession of the latest fashion plates"—"is at a cost which is fast demoralizing the social life of our people," she wrote. "It is an open secret that this love of dress is so strong that many a young woman will barter her soul to obtain it."

With their errant taste and susceptibility to temptation, African American and immigrant women had to be schooled in the ABCs of appropriate attire. How else would they ever learn to wear cotton and wool rather than satin and silk, subdued rather than strong colors, and sensible shoes in place of fancy footwear? How else would they ever learn to dress like Americans? "Perhaps at no time of her adult life is the immigrant girl more impressionable, more sensitive to suggestion, than during her first few months in America," explained Paradise. At that point "American life can mold her as it will." Added one of her colleagues, Lana Bishop of Cleveland's Technical High School, teaching "good taste in dress" was vital to the process of transforming those at the margins of society into "efficient thinkers and workers, homemakers and good citizens." Taking its cue from Paradise, Bishop, and other like-minded social reformers, New York's Hebrew Technical School for Girls was one institution (among many) that sought actively to mold young Jewish immigrant women. In addition to training them in the "effeminate employments" of needlework and typewriting, much of the curriculum was given over to inculcating "a womanly pride in cleanliness and a nicety of personal appointment." The school hewed to a scrupulously maintained dress code in which white middy blouses and heavy black stockings were de rigueur while makeup and excessively stylish clothing were forbidden. The school's well-bred instructors also taught by personal example. Their "ladylike demeanor, gentleness, dignity and modesty" inspired those under their wing to be ladies at all times. Indeed, the teachers were so prim and proper, recalled one graduate, "you would think they were nuns."

Meanwhile, instructors at the New Jersey Manual Training and Industrial School in Bordentown, where most of the students were African Americans, made a point of adding lessons on the "principles of color selection" and the "skillful use of color" to the standard vocational curriculum to wean young men and women away from what was perceived as a collective predilection for bold reds, oranges, greens, and yellows. Students needed to learn "that people dress in order to make a picture and that to make a beautiful picture the correct colors must be combined in the right proportion," declared educator Teresa Staats. It was important that "Negro children understand the relation between the color of their clothing and the color of their skins"—in other words, that they avoid flamboyance in their attire. Negro children, Staats believed, should not stand out. At Fisk University, too, much emphasis was placed on how African American college students dressed—far too much, insisted W. E. B. Du Bois, taking aim at the way the school "sneers and raves and passes all sorts of rules against the overdressing of its students." With so much ugliness around them, was it any wonder that so many of them "flame in their clothing? That they desire to fill their starved souls with overuse of silk and color?" Excessive legislation was not the way to go, he argued: to "inculcate good taste in dress is a far more subtle matter than stiff rules and harsh judgements." Preaching tolerance rather than repression, Du Bois nevertheless believed that good taste in fashion benefited the African American community. E. Azalia Hackley, author of *The Colored Girl Beautiful,* an advice manual, went a step further. Properly channeled, fashion could even be a source of moral uplift, she counseled her readers. Although "few colored women can afford to keep up with the pace of styles," they could learn to dress simply, to cultivate the "laws of proportion," and, above all, to practice self-control, for "culture *is* self-control."

Hackley had it right. Fashion was now the ultimate test of character—for all Americans. Pitting discipline and restraint against desire, fashion demanded a lot of its followers. To be à la mode was one thing; to be under Dame Fashion's thumb was quite another. Perhaps that's why one of the nation's leading fashion authorities, Mary Brooks Picken, thought it a good idea for the American woman to make the following declaration before she went shopping:

A Pledge for the American Woman

As an American woman, I pledge myself to strive always to acquire and wear only such clothes as are appropriate and individually becoming; to avoid extremes in design and color; to respect my clothes enough to care for them to the best of my ability; and to select my clothes so that, in fairness to them, they may give back to me in service more than they cost me in money.

Armed with this pledge, every American woman could step into a department store or a dress shop confident that fashion was her friend, not her undoing.

CHARM

As much a force of nature as a business venture, fashion intoxicated the senses.

CHAPTER TWO

Down with the Corset and Up with the Hemline!

When it came to studying the "feminine personality," there was no better place than the dress department of a large store, suggested sociologist Frances Donovan in 1929. Having spent several months "undercover" selling clothing, she had discovered how fundamentally similar one female shopper was to another. "They come from the wealthiest homes, from middle-class apartments and from the tenements. . . . They are Americans, Europeans, Orientals, Ethiopians. Many can scarcely speak English but, when they buy dresses, they are astonishingly alike." Every one of them wanted to be pretty. Central to America's definition of womanliness, at least since the mid-nineteenth century, prettiness was widely celebrated as a woman's "birthright," even her duty. While the specifics of how to dress prettily changed often—sleeves billowed, then narrowed; hats sported one feather rather than two; colors turned from heliotrope to pastel pink—its lineaments remained remarkably constant well into the 1920s. As much a kinetic concept as a physical one, prettiness entailed shapeliness and ornamentality, roundness and grace, repose and containment. C. H. Crandall, writing on women's fashions in the *North American Review,* lyrically described it as that "flowing outline that shall proclaim at once the sweetness and preciousness of womanhood." Prettiness, then, was womanliness to the nth degree.

But by the end of the nineteenth century, this vision of loveliness was coming under attack. Entering the public sphere in growing numbers, many women began to question the relevance of sweetness and preciousness to their own lives. Whether styling themselves New Women in the 1890s or feminists two decades later, they sought the "beauty of a free personality." In search of an expanded self, some women took to politics, others to writing, and still others, in a gesture at once intimate and bold, to styles of dress different from their mothers' and grandmothers'. The shape of a blouse and the length of a skirt now signaled what kind of woman one wanted to be: ornamental, active, or a little bit of both.

For all its virtues, womanliness came at a price, as any nineteenth-century American woman could attest. With its pounds of fabric, "shin-swaddling flounces," and tightly laced corsets, women's clothing was difficult to wear. Hard to keep clean, milady's skirts weighed a ton, making it difficult for her to get about; her corset, an elaborate concoction of whalebone and steel, kept her upright as a statue while her gloves—which no self-respecting lady was without—kept the outside world at arm's length. As for her hats, she was all too often at the mercy of her milliner, who, it was said, treated a woman's head "as a mere rotary ball" upon which to perch whatever she pleased, "be it bird of paradise or beast or

When cosseted and corseted, American women were likened to latter-day muses.

creeping thing." When conventionally attired like this, a pretty woman was the very picture of contained verticality, of mobility held in check. Or, as Frances Willard, the temperance leader, hotly put it, woman was a "creature born to the beauty and the freedom of Diana, but she is swathed by her skirts, splintered by her stays, bandaged by her tight waist and pinioned by her sleeves until—alas, that I should live to say it!—a trussed turkey or a spitted goose are her most appropriate emblems."

Not every member of the fairer sex docilely accepted her "whalebone thralldom." As early as the 1850s, for instance, progressive women like Elizabeth Cady Stanton and Amelia Bloomer shortened their skirts to four or five inches below the knee and donned baggy Turkish trousers in protest against the oppressive physical and cultural weight of contemporary female attire. "We only wore it because we found it comfortable, convenient, safe and tidy," Bloomer later recalled of the ensemble the press eponymously dubbed "bloomers." She and the others had "no thought of introducing a fashion." Still, quite a number of women were sufficiently inspired by Bloomer and Stanton's example to form a Dress Reform Association and to sponsor a convention in 1857 to discuss the "question of American costume." Their intention, explained Jennie Croly, one of the convention's organizers, was not to advocate any "outré notions or to subvert" present-day styles. What they wanted, she said, was the right to decide "what we will not wear." In the years that followed, dress reform became a casualty of the Civil War, only to resurface briefly in the 1870s with the publication of a number of medically minded tracts on the "calculable injury" that women's attire wrought on the body.

By the turn of the century, "dress-protestants" came into their own. Harnessing science and the new "antisepticonsciousness" to the cause of sartorial reform, they attempted to make newly fashion-conscious women equally aware of the germs and dirt particles that lodged in the hemlines of their stylishly long skirts. "The

Practical devices like this one enabled women to navigate the streets.

streets of our great cities are not kept as clean as they should be, and probably will not be kept scrupulously clean until automobiles have entirely replaced horse-drawn vehicles," observed *Scientific American*, a "weekly journal of practical information, art, science, mechanics, chemistry and manufactures." Women swept the streets with their skirts, taking with them "abominable filth . . . which is by courtesy called 'dust.'" Other detractors, less constrained by good manners, actually took to cataloging the contents of the so-called septic skirt and found that it housed several cigar ends and cigarette butts, a couple of stray hairpins, a few desultory pieces of orange peel, and even a forkful of pork pie! Still others blamed the unsanitary conditions of the street on men's vulgar habit of spitting. "If men were compelled to don skirts for a while, I think their expectorations would soon stop," wrote the editor of the *Ladies' Home Journal* in 1897, urging men to put themselves in a woman's place. "But," he added realistically,

CORSETS AND CORSET WAISTS.

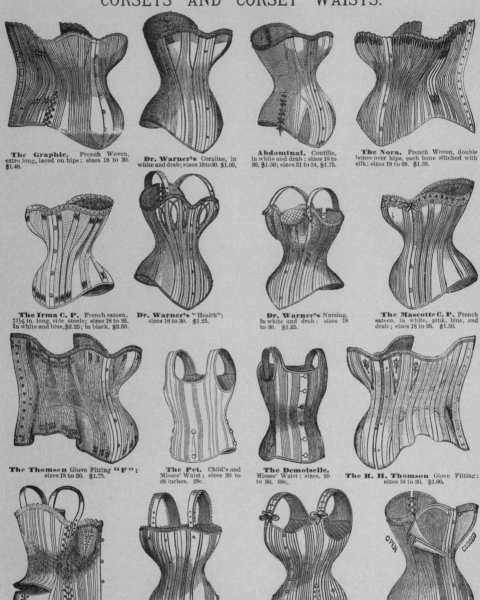

The Graphic. French Woven, extra long, laced on hips; sizes 18 to 30. $1.48.

Dr. Warner's Coraline, in white and drab; sizes 18 to 30. $1.00.

Abdominal. Coutille, in white and drab; sizes 18 to 30, $1.50; sizes 31 to 34, $1.75.

The Nora. French Woven, double bones over hips, each bone stitched with silk; sizes 18 to 28. $1.39.

The Irma C. P. French sateen, 11½ in. long, side steels; sizes 18 to 26. In white and blue, $2.25; in black, $2.50.

Dr. Warner's "Health"; sizes 18 to 30. $1.25.

Dr. Warner's Nursing, in white and drab; sizes 18 to 30. $1.25.

The Mascotte C. P. French sateen, in white, pink, blue, and drab; sizes 18 to 26. $1.50.

The Thomson Glove Fitting "F"; sizes 18 to 30. $1.75.

The Pet. Child's and Misses' Waist; sizes 20 to 28 inches. 29c.

The Demoiselle. Misses' Waist; sizes, 20 to 30. 69c.

The R. H. Thomson Glove Fitting; sizes 18 to 30. $1.00.

Madame Foy's Improved Corset and Skirt Supporter; sizes 18 to 30. 89c.

The Pearl. Misses' Corset; steels in front, in white and drab; sizes 18 to 28. 39c.

The Vera. Ladies' Waist; sizes 18 to 30. $1.43.

The Comfort Nursing; sizes 18 to 30. $1.19.

French Hand-made Satin Corsets, in all colors, $4.25, $5.00, $6.35 to $25.00.

Ranging in style, corsets served the "individual requirements" of every woman.

"as such a change is not probable, it behooves every man to do what he can to correct the habit in other ways."

Mother Nature, meanwhile, exacerbated matters. In 1895, a group of women constituting themselves the Rainy Day Club, took to the sidewalks of New York to demonstrate against the "hobbling, crippling impediment of dry goods dragging" at their feet, which, when wet and dirty, made them catch cold. Clad in a special "rainy day" costume of their own devising—a full skirt some four inches off the ground, complemented by a "pert, little short-tailed" jacket and a jaunty Alpine hat—the Rainy Daisies, as they were known, created quite a stir. "Just four inches from the floor!" reported the *Times* with considerable excitement. "But it startled the whole country. Women had participated in the fight for suffrage and the abolition of slavery. True, a few dress reformers had declared that women should wear bloomers, but they were dismissed as fanatics and there the matter dropped, but for a group to come out in positive approval of short skirts—and four inches from the floor—had never happened before."

Where the Rainy Daisies focused the nation's attention on skirt lengths, most advocates of what was variously called "correct," "rational," or "improved" dress (the latter was the preferred term; it sounded less "aggressive") reserved their greatest disdain for the corset. "The corset-curse among women is more insidious than the drink-curse among men," hotly declared dress reformer Helen Ecob, author of the popular advice book *The Well-Dressed Woman: A Study in the Practical Application to Dress of the Laws of Health, Art and Morals.* "A woman can no more be trusted with a corset than a drunkard with a glass of

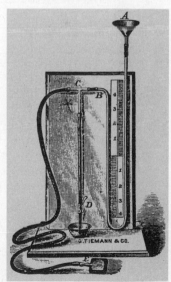

The "manometer" measured the impact of the corset on the female frame.

whiskey." Reinforcing a woman's allegedly natural inclinations toward helplessness, the corset also made her ill. Virtually everything that ailed womankind was attributed to the corset's tight stays, from poor posture and "feeble muscular power" to pelvic disturbances and the "fretfulness, ill-temper and peevishness that darkens many households."

Dress reformers liked to tell grim, "mostly autobiographical" tales of how corsets transformed healthy, fleet-flooted, energetic young women into willowy yet listless specimens of femininity. They also liked to punctuate their lectures and publications with frightening illustrations of distorted body parts—oversize livers, protruding stomachs, squished rib cages, and swaying spines—as well as with "data" drawn from the frontiers of modern medical science. Ecob, for instance, drew heavily on the work of Dr. Robert L. Dickinson, whose newly invented "manometer" measured the amount of pressure that a corset exerted on a woman's upper body. Using a scale and a glass tube filled with mercury, the Brooklyn doctor ascertained that the weight of even the loosest corset approximated that of a twenty-five-pound sack of flour.

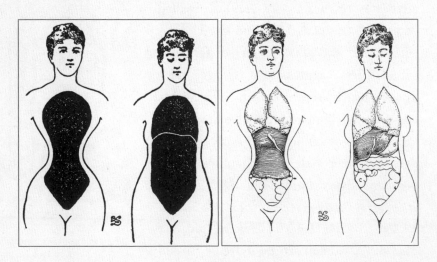

Drawings of displaced viscera brought home the ill effects of tight lacing.

"How many women can carry a sack of flour?" Such constant pressure on the vital organs, Dickinson and his fellow physicians deduced, was harmful in the extreme, making for shallow breathing, a rapid heartbeat, constipation, irritability, and cowardice. Some reformers, like Willard, went so far as to hold corsets accountable for stupidity as well. "Niggardly waists and niggardly brains go together," she wrote, noting that "a ligature around the vital organs at the smallest diameter of the womanly figure means an impoverished blood supply in the brain, and may explain why women scream when they see a mouse."

Dress reformers not only fulminated against the ills of traditional female attire but sought to correct them as well. Insisting that modern-day women had "no use for fashion-plates" and did not covet the "stiff pantaloonery of masculine attire," the champions of rational dress tried their hand at designing a garment that would mediate between the excesses of women's fashion on the one hand and the constraints of the male wardrobe on the other. In search of comfortable clothing appropriate to their sex, they looked to the classical world for sartorial inspiration. Like the ancient Greeks, they took simplicity as their byword: women's dress, they maintained, ought to be "unburdensome and unshackling" as well as "dirt-escapable and pocket-accessible." The corset, of course, was the first item of female clothing to be discarded. Consign it to a museum and class it "with the ancient instruments of torture," suggested dress reformer Grace Greenwood in 1892. Ecob had much the same idea, telling her readers to throw away their corsets and stifle any "lingering penchant for whalebone. The destruction of the corset must go to the roots, branch and remotest twig." Even "incipient corsets," the thick, heavily corded waists worn by young girls, had to be abandoned. Greenwood, Ecob, and their followers touted the merits of either the "health waist," essentially a loose-fitting undershirt fastened with buttons, or the one-piece union suit, which reached from the

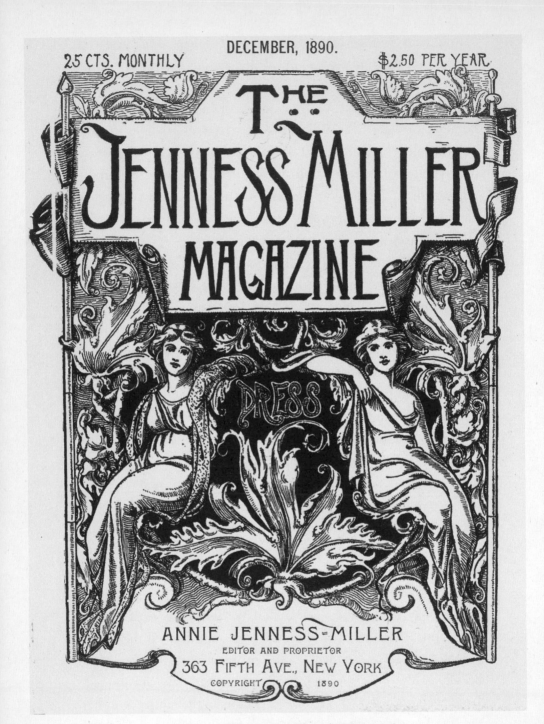

The *Jenness Miller Magazine* was dedicated to the
"high and holy mission" of dress reform.

neck almost to the ankle, encasing each leg separately. Made of "elastic weave," the union suit had the virtue of clinging to the entire body while allowing it to move freely.

As for outerwear, seekers of sensible dress were encouraged to don a simple, loose-fitting garment whose origins stretched as far back as antiquity and as far away as the East. Where conventional women's attire, with its seams and darts, thrust the breasts out and emphasized the shoulders so that the body resembled an "inverted cone," or hourglass, its alternative was literally of a piece. Filmy and flowing, it fell seamlessly from top to bottom. An adaptation of the tunic, this "charming gown," enthused an admirer, did not "cramp the chest or impound the heart or trespass on the stomach." Women also had the option of wearing a version of the traditional ladies' exercise costume, which combined a blouse and a pair of pantaloons, or so-called Turkish trousers. Both ensembles were entirely stripped of ornament, of froufrou and feathers, of the "button that buttoned nothing and the bow that tied nothing."

Not surprisingly, many women had to be coaxed to try this novel form of dressing. Wouldn't they be too cold? Or look untidy? they wondered. "I am very stout," said one woman, not too keen on the prospect of relinquishing her corset. Without it, "I should look like a tub." Ecob was quick to reassure her. "It is no worse to look like a tub than an hour-glass," she said. "You will move more easily, and therefore your size will be less apparent, if your clothing is loose. Of two evils, choose the lesser." Taking its cue from Ecob, the *American Jewess,* a magazine for middle-class American Jewish women, recommended to its readers that when cleaning house, they might consider retiring their corsets for an hour or two. "Off with the corsets, while working, I say. Just try it, ladies, and then tell me how you like it."

Younger women seemed to like it a great deal, as did those moving into the larger life of the modern world: working women

SCIENTIFIC SYSTEM OF DRESS FOR WOMEN.

The Famous Divided Skirt

— OR —

TURKISH LEGLETTES.

OUR SILK SKIRTS ARE MADE OF THE CELEBRATED CUTTER SILK FABRICS.

"Beauty and Health are the Birthright of every Woman."
—ANNIE JENNESS MILLER.

This renowned undergarment is superseding the old-time clumsy petticoat wherever women consult beauty, grace, and health, in the fashion of their apparel.

Dresses fall over the divided skirt more gracefully than over old-fashioned undergarments.

No bulk, no weight, no tight bands, no shoulder straps, no clumsiness.

A true hygienic garment which is an aid to beauty.

Perfect freedom of movement. No lady who wears the Turkish Leglettes could be induced to wear petticoats again.

Many of the best-dressed and most eminent leaders of society have adopted the divided skirt.

The demand for the Divided Skirt and plain Winter Leglettes has become so great that we are now manufacturing them on a large scale at the following prices:

PRICE LIST
JENNESS-MILLER DIVIDED SKIRTS.

Pride of the West, plain,	$2.00
" " " trimmed,	$2.50 to $5.00
Worsted Pongee,	$1.50
Mohair (according to quality),	$2.25 to $3.50
Cambric, plain,	$2.00
King Philip Cambric, or Pride of West Muslin,	$2.50 upw'd
" " " trim'd,	$3.00 "
All Wool Flannel Cloth,	$2.50
Fine French Flannel,	$3.50 to $5.50
Very fine Mohair, in black, white, and gray,	$3.50 to $5.50
Cashmere, all colors,	$4.00 upward
Pongee Silk, natural color, plain,	$5.50
" " " " briar stitched,	$7.00
J. D. Cutter Silk, black or white,	$10.00
" " " " briar stitched,	$11.50
Fine Satin Surah, all colors, except black,	$8.00 upward
China Silk, plain,	$9.00
" " briar stitched,	$10.50
Pongee Silk, accordion plaited,	$12.50
China " "	$20.00
" " " with ribbon,	$23.00 to $25.00
J. D. Cutter Silk Skirt, interlined French Flannel,	$12.50
" " " " briar stitch,	$15.00
No. 2510, Knit, short, black, white, gray, or red,	$3.50
" 2520, " medium,	$3.50
" 2530, " "	$4.00
" 2540, " long,	$4.50

In ordering send waist measure and length.

THE JENNESS-MILLER DIVIDED SKIRT.

This illustration represents an Accordion Plaited Divided Skirt; it is an improvement over every other means for clothing the legs underneath the dress skirt. With this garment one gets a minimum of weight with a maximum of warmth, while the freedom in the use of these necessary members is a great argument in favor of a bifurcated garment, and for cleanliness, convenience, comfort, and safety in traveling about these garments are preferable to the traditional petticoat.

THE CHEMILETTE,

THREE GARMENTS IN ONE.

THIS IS THE MOST ELEGANT AND CONVENIENT UNDERGARMENT EVER INVENTED.

WE MANUFACTURE THEM IN THE FOLLOWING MATERIALS.

Pride of the West, plain,	$2 00
" " " trimmed,	$2 50 to 7 00
King Philip Cambric, plain,	2 00
King Philip Cambric, lace trimmed,	$2 50 to 7 00
Pongee Silk, plain,	5 00
Pongee Silk, briar stitched and lace trimmed,	7 50
Surah Silk, plain,	6 00
Surah Silk, stitched and trimmed,	8 00
China Silk, plain,	8 00
China Silk, stitched and trimmed,	10 00
French Flannel, plain,	4 00
French Flannel, stitched and trimmed,	5 50
Cashmere, lace trimmed,	6 00

THE JENNESS-MILLER MFG. DEPARTMENT, 363 Fifth Avenue, New York.

Dress reformers believed that "chic and elegance" could be attained by avoiding "forced, unnatural" forms of attire.

and "wheelwomen" (as bicyclists and sports enthusiasts were called), the college-bound and "college-bred" who took pride in being "something more than fashion plates or ornaments." Octavia Bates, an alumna of the University of Michigan, was among those who embraced "healthful and sensible" dress. Traditional female attire, she claimed, slowed women down, mentally as well as physically, and placed female undergraduates like her at a considerable disadvantage. The weight of women's clothing, Bates wrote, was a "constant drain upon the nervous force" and impeded the freedom of motion necessary for "using instruments and heavy dictionaries, [and] for doing blackboard work." It was no wonder that "some girls break down in health, under all this stress and strain."

Salvation, though, was within reach of one's closet, provided you had the right clothes. "What if, some morning, the college girls from their gymnasia, and the numerous physical culture classes in our cities, should appear on our streets, by common consent, dressed in a modified form of the gymnasium suit?" asked one veteran dress reformer. "The high school girls would follow the college girls, and the clerks, typewriters, and all working girls would be with them, and you and I, with gray in our hair, would soon join in the glad procession, little girls of all sizes skipping in freedom by our sides." Not everyone found the prospect delightful. Men were especially quick to ridicule women clad in "gym suits" and other forms of rational dress, subjecting them to rude stares and vulgar comment. But then, women could be just as hostile. "While the men opposed us at every turn," recalled a founder of the Rainy Daisies, "it was difficult to say which were our worst enemies, the men or the women. . . . We found it pretty hard to persuade women that short skirts were hygienic and pretty." An anonymous editorial writer for *Harper's Bazaar* was characteristic of those who needed to be persuaded. "A short-skirted woman on the street, except in a deluge of rain, is a blow to one's ideals. The older the woman, the

Reformers frowned on cinched waists.

greater the blow," she wrote with mounting indignation. Conceding that the warnings of science were not to be taken lightly, the journalist nevertheless entered a plea for long skirts. What happened when you reduced dress to a "grim assurance of public health"? Didn't "women's mission to be lovely" matter any longer?

Comments like these suggest just how much of an uphill battle the reformers faced. Those opposed, and their numbers were legion, made use of a sizable repertoire of reasons to keep women corseted and covered. Some, equating the corset with civic virtue, insisted that its removal would weaken the national character. America was nothing if not a "corset-wearing nation," they claimed. Others, equating sensible attire with an "artless announcement of indifference to appearance," objected on aesthetic grounds. "Lovely woman has no right to war upon beauty or propriety," cautioned the *American Jewess* in July 1895, encouraging its readers to stay clear of bloomers, which were ugly and had "a tendency to reveal what ought to be hidden." When, several months later, there was talk of erecting a statue honoring Amelia Bloomer in full regalia, the magazine recoiled in horror. "A woman in bloomers speeding along on a bicycle is a sorry enough spectacle," without immortalizing her in marble. "Drape Mrs. Amelia in a couple of sheets and a cameo breast-pin and I am with you to the limits of my income, but for stone bloomers—nary a cent. Millions for art—not one cent for grotesqueness!" Still others objected on practical grounds, noting how it made little sense for a businesswoman to sit at her desk dressed as if she were a classical statue: "We must look in some other direction than the bloomer costume or Roman togas for a solution." And then, of course, there were women who no doubt preferred the dictates of fashion to the dictates of science or, alternatively, liked things just the way they were and actually enjoyed lacing themselves into their corsets. "The majority of women are really as indifferent to art as they are to health and everything else in

Billowing sleeves also occasioned dismay.

connection with dress," related one exasperated reformer. "Their one and only desire is to be thought 'smart.'"

Implicit throughout was the fear that rational dressing robbed women of their femininity. The "affectation of queer or freakish dressing does not belong to a normal woman," charged its detractors, intimating that clothing that failed to conform to the regnant aesthetic of prettiness was downright deviant. Associating dress reform either with "hoydenish" girls or "mannish middle-aged and old ladies," its opponents believed that Turkish trousers and corsetless bodies constituted a departure from womanliness. To their way of thinking, dress reform called up a "vision of short hair, knee skirts, and high laced bicycle boots . . . of mannish cravats, and severe coats and skirts." It didn't have to, of course. Rational, sensible dress could be graceful, delightful, even comely, insisted its devotees. But most Americans failed to see it that way.

The sleek geometry of the flapper's clothes broke radically with tradition.

Instead, they clung to a static, timeless ideal of womanliness that held that female dress had to reflect "woman's mission to make life gentler and more beautiful."

In time, styles picked up where high-minded dress reformers left off, making mobility and ease fashionable. While it took a while before women shortened their skirts and loosened their stays—first, they had to pass through the "trials" of the hobble skirt—by the early 1920s, "abbreviated" skirts, short hair, and a lean sil-

Baring a little or a lot, these clothes gently enclosed the body.

houette had become "accomplished facts." In the "new era of undressing" that was the Roaring Twenties a new woman was born. Dubbed "Flapper Jane," she worked for a living, played golf and tennis, drove a car, and liked to smoke and drink. She also liked to wear "two-ounce underthings" beneath her stylish outfits. A peep into her closet revealed a whole new world—or, as a member of that generation put it, the "clothes chronicle of the woman of 1920–29 tells a different story and tells it eloquently": how Flapper Jane broke with tradition by sundering prettiness from womanliness.

For one thing, the corset, previously indispensable, had finally become about as "dead as the dodo's grandfather." Among the younger set, it "rode low on the Ferris wheel of fashion," Fannie Hurst noted, cleverly alluding to the new Ferris brand of female undergarments. Even those ill-prepared completely to jettison their corsets could find ones that fit "naturally," like the "Sportelette" made by the Treo-Elastic Company or the corsets made by H. W. Gossard, whose undergarments "idealized" the body. Gossard corsets, it was said, would "do more for your figure than you dare hope. They give the graceful carriage of youth. And youth is always in style." Gone, too, were the cumbersome dresses of yesteryear. "We choose them slim and short," declared the *Ladies' Home Journal* in 1925. "As American women are noted for their pretty feet and ankles, it is pleasant to learn that skirts are going to be very short—fourteen inches from the ground is the truly correct length, though one must adjust length to becomingness."

Weight, circumstance, and age also figured in the new calculus of "becomingness." Large women, for example, were advised never to wear anything too short. "Whatever fashion may dictate to her petite sister," six to eight inches from the ground was considered the outer limit for the stylish stout. Working women were also enjoined to keep their skirts at a respectable length. "Being smartly and appropriately frocked for the office," chided a leading fashion magazine, "is almost as much the business woman's job as attending to letters and answering questions and the woman of today is quick to realize that much of her success depends upon correct office clothes." Mothers, too, were encouraged to dress "correctly" by wearing skirts that were longer than their daughters' and more in keeping with their age. All too often, though, such advice went unheeded. "Ten years ago," reported the *Chicago Tribune* in 1928, "women still had ages. . . . Today mother and daughter may be found any time in the junior department supplementing their wardrobes from the same racks." More to the point,

The modern woman had fewer clothes to launder than her grandmother.

observed the daily, every successful designer needed to operate on the assumption that "all American women are young" and eternally in search of "girlish grace."

Flapper Janes of all ages now flattened their breasts, hid their hips, and put on silk stockings. Striding down the street, "regiment" after "regiment of beige-colored legs" radiated a new kind of womanliness, easy and unfettered. "We can now dodge autos with a step, a real step backward or forward. . . . We can get on and off a [street] car without taking Brodie's leap or having to be

lifted off like a child. We can take a few 'manly' strides when trying to catch a train and not mince along like those of our Chinese
sisters who still cling to old traditions." Practical considerations
aside, short skirts were also said to be artistic and a bit daring. By
wearing an abbreviated skirt, reported one well-disposed male
eyewitness, many women were able to "express a modern inner
urge that manifests in other women in the form of drinking and
smoking. Even in the small places where for any woman to be
known as a drinker or a smoker means social ostracism, the short
skirt is passed by the local Mrs. Grundys with hardly more than a
sniff." A few Mrs. Grundys had even taken to wearing one themselves. Clearly, the short skirt was here to stay.

Or was it? Hailed by some as a badge of freedom and modernity, short skirts were just as likely to be condemned as an assault
on womanliness. It was as if the younger generation had forgotten the meaning of modesty, one traditionally minded woman
told the *Times*, suggesting that the word might as well "be taken
out of the dictionary." In fact, the higher hemlines climbed, the
more tempers flared. In Evanston, Illinois, for example, the
young men of the local Congregational church pledged "never to
speak or walk with any girl wearing short skirts," forcing a number of young couples to break up, while in Vinland, Kansas, the
parents of two young schoolgirls sued the local school board for
refusing to let their daughters shorten their skirts. If they had to,
vowed the girls' parents, they'd take the case all the way to the
Supreme Court. Meanwhile, in Los Angeles, Ruth D. Howland
sued her husband for divorce on the grounds that he forced her to
wear long skirts. Mr. Howland made her wear her skirts down to
her ankles and she wanted to wear them to her knees, she told the
court. "Was that cruelty?" queried the presiding judge. "It was to
me," she replied.

In and out of court, disgruntled Americans like Mr. Howland
made common cause against the short skirt, whose skimpiness

they associated with a precipitous decline in standards of womanly comportment. Throughout the 1920s, they were joined by an unusual coalition of doctors, dress manufacturers, society women, and churchmen determined to consign contemporary fashions to the attic. It was up to them to "swing the pendulum of styles and manners back toward an age of purity, piety and the elusive ankle," they insisted. "We must do something about those knees!" Something more fundamental than aesthetic issues was hanging in the balance: the essence of the modern American woman. Was she to be dainty and demure or sleek and assertive? A paragon of modesty or of modernity?

In the campaign against knees, medicine was one useful ally. "Scantiness in modern women's dress is partly responsible for the tuberculosis problem," sweepingly declared Dr. Hoye E. Dearholt, the head of a Wisconsin sanatorium. "Girls, between 15 and 25, striving for a boyish figure and wearing scanty clothing have lowered their resistance to the point where they are easy prey of the disease." Though the *New York Times,* for one, dismissed this statement and others like it out of hand, arguing that the "assumption that such exposures are dangerous rests on no study of vital statistics," the critics of scanty clothing had few compunctions about making their claims. The short skirt, they insisted, was harmful to one's health. Others indicted the short skirt for its chilling effect on the economy. As the need for fabric dropped—only seven yards were needed to make a "flapper uniform," compared with the nineteen or twenty yards for an outfit produced in, say, 1913—textile production dropped markedly as well. Calling for a "renaissance of the long skirt," manufacturers throughout the nation sought to persuade American women to return to petticoats and long skirts . . . to meet the crisis in the industry. "Of all the absurd suggestions!" responded Harriot T. Cooke. "The naive idea that women should be so altruistic as to increase the cost of their clothing by using more material, forego much of their comfort and give up their smart appearance just to help along one brand of trade is most amusing."

But then, the critics of short skirts were not easily amused. Modern-day fashions, they insisted, not only damaged the physical and economic health of the nation but loosened its moral underpinnings as well—and that simply couldn't be countenanced, especially by women of good breeding and high social standing like Mrs. John B. Henderson. A prominent Washington, D.C., hostess known for her teetotaling vegetarian dinners, this straitlaced and "straight-backed, gracious little lady of seventy-odd years" publicly appealed to the Daughters of the American Revolution, the National Federation of Women's Clubs, and women's colleges throughout the country to campaign against short skirts. Women like her, she said, must "band together to condemn such vulgar fashions of women's apparel that do not tend to cultivate innate modesty, good taste or good morals," lest they fall prey to "physical bankruptcy and race degeneracy." With so much at stake, Henderson's crusade generated considerable interest. "It really is amazing how much agitating the campaign has aroused," she proudly told a reporter. "Letters deluge me every day . . . from teachers and clergymen, despairing mothers and irate swains." Though heartened by the show of support, the Washington socialite was considerably frustrated by the slow pace of sartorial change. For all her efforts, she conceded, "Paris has not lowered the flag by the width of a hairpin . . . and American women are out-Parising Paris." Still, Mrs. Henderson remained unbowed and undefeated, telling her supporters a year later, "it is not beyond the realm of possibility that [my] resolutions may start a real craze of reform . . . and may mark the start of a new era in our modes and manners."

America's religious leaders shared Mrs. Henderson's vision and labored mightily throughout the 1920s to convince their flocks that flapper fashion was indecent. As the Salvation Army, invoking history, vividly put it, the "skirt that trails in the dirt gathering germs is a menace to its wearer's health; but the skirt that flaps around the knees is pretty much of a menace to the modesty of the women who wear it." The modern church and synagogue were certainly no strangers to sartorial issues. Religious prescriptive literature was replete with admonitions to young girls to "free themselves from the yoke of Fashion" by making modesty their "bosom friend." Sermons, in turn, routinely took adults to task for their "love of finery and passion for dress," exhorting them to bear in mind that it was not a "disgrace to be seen in the same garment more than once." In the twenties, though, ecclesiastic vexation with fashion mounted as America's ministers, priests, and rabbis, horrified by what they saw on the streets and in the pews (all those knees!), actively sought to prevent their stylishly clad congregants from losing their souls, as well as their wallets, to Dame Fashion. Though some Americans thought such attempts at sartorial control were ultimately futile—"All the precepts of earth and even of Heaven will change nothing. . . . Women will always do what they want to do and, above all, what other people don't want them to do"—religious leaders were undeterred in their efforts to promote and sustain a timeless vision of womanliness.

A popular sermon topic, the "glaring immodesty" of contemporary clothing inspired clergymen like Rabbi Stephen S. Wise of New York's Free Synagogue and Dr. John Roach Straton, pastor of Calvary Baptist Church, to new oratorical heights. Wise devoted his 1922 New Year's address to inveighing against the "follies and sins" that "deformed society"—among them, "decadent manners, improper dress," and the way young women "openly" used cosmetics. Sounding awfully like Mrs. Henderson, he exclaimed: "What can we expect from the people of Grand Street and Houston Street [the immigrant Jewish residents of the Lower East Side] when they see such examples as these? Rottenness comes from the top." Straton, for his part, mockingly used humor to make a similar point, composing a ditty entitled "Mary's Little Skirt":

> Mary had a little skirt,
> The latest style, no doubt,
> But every time she got inside
> She was more than halfway out.

Rabbis might thunder and pastors break into song, but neither came close to matching the Catholic clergy in its fierce and uncompromising stand against short skirts. In this, as in so many other instances, America's Catholic Church took its cue from Pope Pius XI, whose tenure as pontiff was marked by "strenuous" opposition to contemporary dress. "Christ Himself would blush at its unseemliness," the pope liked to say, inspiring his followers to denounce short skirts for their "disedifying violations of modesty in dress and Christian propriety of conduct." No "consistent Catholic women," the church insisted, "would wear them." They dishonored Catholicism's good name.

To be sure, the zeal with which America's clergymen railed against contemporary fashions had much to do with the makeup of their congregants, a disproportionately large number of whom were women. "I like to go to church. It's the only place, about, I ever do go," acknowledged one married Middletown woman. "Religion hasn't anything to do with it," added one of her younger contemporaries. "We go where the boys are." Whatever their motivations, women filled the pews of churches and synagogues everywhere. Dressed in their best, in smart, "knowing" hats, tailored suits, pretty dresses, and kid gloves with tiny pearl buttons, they sought communion with God and with one another; the chance to hone their sartorial senses was an added bonus. "It may perchance seem irrelevant to consider fashion in connection with church," observed fashion maven Mary Brooks Picken, encouraging American women to pay attention to what their fellow worshipers wore. "How many times at Sunday dinner, when the text of the sermon has been discussed, does not some member of the family say, 'Did you notice what a pretty dress or hat Miss or Mrs. So and So had on this morning?' " "Church-going women folk," she noted approvingly, "evidence splendid taste in dress and . . . the clothes they wear are excellent style criterions."

Those in the pulpit, though, brought a different perspective to bear. Appealing directly to "all truly Catholic ladies to take up the fight," the church called on them to be "living tabernacles" rather than fashion plates. "It is so easy to fall in with the crowd—to be in style," acknowledged *Ave Maria,* a popular Catholic family magazine. But Catholics were expected to live their lives according to a different set of rules: a good Catholic not only acted like one but looked like one, too. Mindful of their duty, men were also enlisted in the "war against immodest dress." "Fathers, sons and husbands," the pontiff stated in a 1927 address, eager to enlist them as his very own "morality police," should monitor what their women wore and place them under "moral and economic boycott" if they put on something "fashionable but unbecoming."

When public appeals fell short, Catholics took up the tape measure. "Skirts are not to be more than twelve or fifteen inches from the ground, depending upon the height of the girl. Skirts are to be pleated or otherwise made to afford ample fullness," priests, nuns, and parochial-school teachers proclaimed, issuing detailed bulletins by the score. Leaving nothing to chance, members of the church hierarchy closely observed girls kneeling at prayer to see how much fabric covered their knees. American Catholics were by no means alone in their determination to measure decency. "Wear longer skirts and win a badge," declared the All-Chicago Kiwanis Club, inviting girls whose skirts hung not less than twelve inches from the ground to apply for an "emblem of honor." The Salvation Army, meanwhile, proclaimed a "back to normalcy drive," decreeing that the "skirts of Salvation Army lassies must not be more than 7 inches above street level." And in Chattanooga, the Reverend W. C. Robertson of Christ Episcopal Church offered this bit of fashion advice to prospective brides: the sleeves of their wedding gowns were not to be shorter than the elbow, and the skirt "must not be higher than where the spring of the calf of the leg begins and be wide enough to allow of genuflecting before the blessed sacrament without exposing the calf, much less the knee." Brides found guilty of ignoring his advice, the reverend intimated, might not be allowed to be married in his church.

Few such strategies worked. "The dictates of fashion," reluctantly conceded the *Catholic Citizen,* a Milwaukee paper, "seem to be more influential with the average Christian maid and matron than the counsels of religion." Sister Marie Josie, dean of the College of Saint Elizabeth, concurred, glumly observing that the Catholic collegians she knew appeared to hold the sartorial norms of Catholic womanhood in "almost universal disregard." Still others within the Catholic fold complained about the paradoxical effect of sermons on such matters. Wrote one disheartened priest: "We have heard numbers of sermons in which it was evident that the preacher was thoroughly enjoying his own talk, and the members of the congregation—especially the ones referred to—nearly or quite as much. . . . Would not a sermon on the Blessed Mother or the Little Flower delivered with equal vigor and enthusiasm have produced far better results in promoting modesty?"

As the limits of voluntary compliance became all too obvious, the church launched a campaign of steadily mounting restrictiveness. For starters, preachers were urged by Rome to redouble their efforts to sway the hearts and minds of the female faithful. "With all the vigor of their apostolic zeal," priests were to "endeavor with fatherly kindness, with patience and perseverance to convince [women] of the wrong they are doing, for many of them are slaves to this fashion . . . but do not have the strength to rebel against a tyranny that exploits their modesty as the slave trader does the blood of the slaves." The church proceeded to back up its harsh rhetoric by issuing a series of equally harsh "edicts" prohibiting "unchristian" dress. First, it cautioned women against displaying their arms, legs, or necks when attending religious services or gatherings; those who persisted in doing so would be forbidden to enter the sanctuary. Signs to that effect were posted prominently in church vestibules throughout the land. By 1930, as fashion's hold on its faithful showed little sign of abating, the church embarked on an even more drastic course of action. Pope Pius issued a series of regulations—the "twelve rules of dress"—that culminated in barring the immodestly clad from celebrating the sacraments. "Girls and women who wear immodest dress shall be denied Holy Communion, and shall not be admitted as sponsors at Baptism and Confirmation," declared the church, placing them completely beyond the pale.

Traditionalists within the American Jewish community watched carefully as the church adopted these stringent measures. Some Jews, like the delegates to the 1925 convention of the Union of Orthodox Jewish Congregations of America (UOJCA), a group representing the lay leadership of Orthodox Jewry in the United States, welcomed the measures, commending the Catholics for their resoluteness. In tones reminiscent of the church, the delegates sternly declared that they looked "with disfavor upon the laxity of conduct so greatly prevalent at present and particularly on the manner of attire at present customary among the female sex, which cannot be considered decent and modest." Accordingly, they urged "the daughters of Israel to clothe themselves with proper modesty and in particular the ladies attending services, so as not to conflict with the holiness of the places of worship." The UOJCA went farther still. Acknowledging the growing presence of women in the traditional synagogue, a fairly recent development, it sought their active support: "In view of the great laxity of the time, leading on the part of the 'modern woman' to a marked degree of nudity and bareness in dress, which Judaism decries as unchaste, we urge the Jewish women of this country to take the initiative in encouraging a more modest form of dress, especially when attending synagogue for meditation and prayer." Like their Catholic sisters, observant Jewish women were expected to take up the cudgels in defense of modest dress. It was their duty, something expected of them both as true-blue American women and as stalwart daughters of Israel.

The resolution, however, met with unanticipated opposition. While most UOJCA delegates believed that Judaism had the power as well as the right to tell its followers how to dress, a vocal minority was not so sure. Sartorial choice, it argued, is an individual matter, not a communal one: "A church cannot prescribe women's styles." Unswayed, the UOJCA passed the resolution by an overwhelming margin. Like the American Catholic Church, the leaders of Orthodox Jewry were willing and eager to try their hand at imposing their own notions of style on their followers.

News of the debate quickly made its way from the corridors of the convention to the world at large, prompting the *New York Times* to observe wryly that "powerful forces are in clash when the Catholic Church and the orthodox synagogue unite against present styles in women's clothes." But, it hastened to add, the clash was not between the ecclesiastic authorities on the one hand and the daughters of the church and the daughters of Zion on the other. Rather, this particular conflict pitted the powerful forces of religion, Catholicism as well as Judaism, against that equally "mighty circumstance that goes by the name of Fashion." And Fashion, prophesied the *Times,* would ultimately prevail. "When Fashion speaks, economic forces, social forces, psychological forces, emancipations, progress and all the rest mean nothing. The dressmaker breathes upon them and they are not."

The *Times* was right. As the 1920s came to a close, hemlines descended and short skirts fell from grace. "From morning to night, skirts grow longer," *Vogue* observed in 1927, pronouncing the new length "super-chic." Longer, fuller, and more fitted, women's clothing now harked back to a time when women were "feminine in the most thoroughly traditional sense." The new Parisian styles, reported Mildred Adams, "telescope the years from 1880 to 1915 in one mad jumble of color and form. The only thing you will not see is a straight little one-piece frock. That was the flapper uniform and at the present moment there is nothing deader than a flapper." Religion, though, was not implicated in the flapper's demise. The "goddess of fashion" and her apostles, Parisian couturiers such as Paul Poiret, were responsible. Poiret, for one, now disavowed the short skirt, which he had avidly promoted, saying, "Had the life of a short skirt to live over again, I might have shaped it differently." "Stylish women," the French designer explained, "have been going a little too far and for the past few years woman has lost considerably by want of the mystery which constitutes one of her greatest charms." But enough was enough. Eager to reintroduce women to the mysteries of modesty, he "decreed" that fashionable skirts should "end five inches above the ankle instead of five inches above the knee." "Women," he added, "have everything to gain by this trend of the mode." The Hendersons of the world tended to agree and gratefully welcomed the new styles. "Knees have withdrawn into the mysteries and a good thing, too," one newspaper editorialized. Manufacturers and merchants were equally grateful and quickly filled their stockrooms and windows with the latest fashions.

College girls and veteran feminists, however, had a different response: "Not on your life." A poll conducted among Hunter College students revealed that a whopping 70 percent rebelled against the prospect of wearing longer skirts, prompting one newspaper to observe that never had "so many girls presented

A return to longer skirt lengths pleased some and angered others.

such a united front" on any issue. Branding the long skirt "impracticable, uncomfortable and uneconomical," the undergraduates "hooted" at the idea that it represented a return to femininity. The long skirt represented a return all right—a "long step backward in the progress of women's emancipation." Besides, it was "inconvenient in the subway, impossible to accommodate to the length of a coat and bad in its psychological effect on the wearer because it banishes her sense of freedom and comfort." Rumblings of discontent soon spread from the college campus to the city, where many women, newly accustomed to the "freedom of their limbs," lambasted the new skirt length as an "insidious attempt to lure them back to slavery." Some, like Fannie Hurst, urged women to resist. "Here is one of the most important emancipations of woman in the past twelve years about to go to naught," she wrote in the *New Republic.* " 'Down with the corset and up with the hemline!' should be the slogan of every woman who doesn't want to be bullied into doing something as undesirable as it is unwelcome." Other women penned indignant letters to the newspapers or introduced protest resolutions at organizational meetings, charging that the new styles injured their health and produced a "psychology adverse to the further progress of women." And still others debated "the long and the short of the dress problem" at their business and social clubs. Representatives from *Vogue,* appearing at one such debate, attempted to cool things down by taking a more conciliatory view. Women didn't have to abandon the short skirt, they counseled. Business women could wear it to the office but could "lift themselves out of the workaday atmosphere entirely by wearing the longer dress for social events."

Whether lifting themselves out of the world or planting themselves squarely in it, most American women eventually adjusted their skirts—and their sights—accordingly. Dresses, longer than they were at the beginning of the 1920s but shorter than they were before the war, now covered the knees but not the ankles. As knees retreated from public view, so too did talk of rebellion. What endured, though, were multiple variations on the theme of womanliness. Thanks to the Flapper Janes of the world, consensus on what it took to look and act like a woman broke down in modern America of the interwar years. The traditional model of womanliness cherished by the church, the synagogue, and the Daughters of the American Revolution faced increasingly stiff competition from those who preferred ease to containment, angularity to roundness, spiritedness to dependence. In the end, it all came down to one thing: from this point on, definitions of womanliness would vary as much as hemlines.

The Continental's "Good Clothes"

Copyright 1906 by Hart Schaffner & Marx

MANY men prefer the "regular" overcoat style—the Chesterfield. It has this in its favor—it's correct to wear anywhere. We carry the choicest selection from all the best makers in America.

$15 $18 $20 $22 $25 $28 $30

Equal the best custom made. Our overcoat room is the largest in Boston, and our assortment the greatest in New England.

The CONTINENTAL, Boston's Greatest Clothing Store, Washington and Boylston Sts.

Mass-produced menswear was a handsome alternative to custom tailoring.

CHAPTER THREE

The Mark of a Gentleman

"The sex with which I have the honor to be affiliated labors under a severe handicap," observed journalist Frederick Lewis Allen in 1926. "Nobody writes about our clothes." Allen had a point. When it came to men's fashions, no furious tirades, blistering broadsides, or withering exchanges split the air; even guidebooks were in short supply. "Thousands of pages are written every year to assist our wives, daughters and grandmothers to look younger and more entrancing, but we men," lamented Allen, "have to go it alone." America's reticence on the subject of the masculine wardrobe was easy to explain: there wasn't much to say. Where women's fashions were broadly synonymous with change, male attire seemed static, frozen. The fashions of the sturdier sex appeared to be about as "inflexible as the laws of the Medes and the Persians," related one student of contemporary American clothing practices in 1913; added another, "The movement of men's fashions is glacial."

Whether cast in terms of geology or of ancient history, men's clothing—give or take a detail or two, like pockets—had hardly changed since the invention of the suit in the 1800s. Men had long ago abandoned frills and furbelows in favor of what Anne Hollander calls the "standard masculine civil costume," with its strong, clean lines and absence of ornamentation. The gentleman of yesteryear might have adorned his person with all manner of gewgaws but the modern gentleman eschewed them with a vengeance. Frills did not accord with his sense of responsibility and probity, trustworthiness and solidity. Not everyone, of course, thought the current trend such a good thing. "When men wore satins and laces and ruffles, being handsome was not the minor accomplishment that it is today," editorialized the *New York Times* in 1926. "Except for movie heroes and matinee idols, men nowadays scorn the deliberate struggle for beauty." The National Association of Retail Clothiers and Furnishers, representing the menswear industry, was quick to agree. Even in the modern era, when dressing well was not a demanding exercise, the average American man, it pointed out, did not take great pains with his appearance. He tended to buy a new suit only when his old one wore out. It was high time the common man discovered the "pleasure of being well-dressed."

But such pleasure often eluded him. Far more inclined to make light of clothes than to take them seriously, the average Joe did not reject the idea of gentlemanliness so much as disdain all talk of fashion. Any discussion of what the well-dressed man ought to wear seemed, according to one rueful observer, "to occasion raucous mirth in Seattle, Chicago, New York or New Orleans alike." It made too many red-blooded American men uncomfortable. Try as they might, America's moral arbiters found it difficult to con-

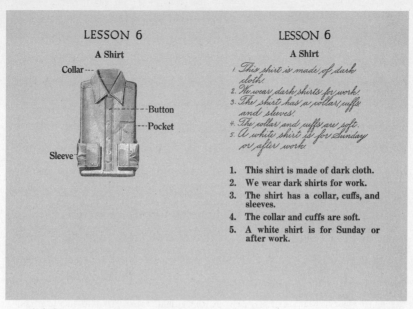

LESSON 6

A Shirt

Collar ---
--- Button
--- Pocket
Sleeve

LESSON 6

A Shirt

1. This shirt is made of dark cloth.
2. We wear dark shirts for work.
3. The shirt has a collar, cuffs, and sleeves.
4. The collar and cuffs are soft.
5. A white shirt is for Sunday or after work.

1. This shirt is made of dark cloth.
2. We wear dark shirts for work.
3. The shirt has a collar, cuffs, and sleeves.
4. The collar and cuffs are soft.
5. A white shirt is for Sunday or after work.

English-language textbooks acquainted immigrants with the fine points of dress as well as of speech.

vince the man on the street that "dressing badly" was not a "sign of intellectual superiority"; most men chose to believe otherwise. From their vantage point, not only was it dumb to pay attention to what one wore, it was foppish or effeminate. As fashion designer and writer Elizabeth Hawes explained in *Men Can Take It,* her breezy account of male attire, American men did not concern themselves too much with clothing lest they be thought "pansies." The "Harvard boys, and the Yale boys and many, many other men and boys all admit it as a factor."

Still, on or off campus, men did care about their clothing; they just didn't talk about it. "If we are honest," said one of their number, "most of us will admit that we admire the meticulously dressed man. His clothes add a certain halo." Rabbi Alexander Kohut of New York no doubt felt that way. The opportunity, every other year, to purchase a new silk-lined frock coat was a much-anticipated event for the rabbi and his family. Proceeding downtown, his wife and children in tow, Rabbi Kohut would lovingly touch the bolts of satin, silk, and wool laid out before him, much like "a musician softly caressing his beloved piano keys." The supple beauty of the fabric, his wife recalled, "beguiled" him. Laymen like Mr. Wolfson, the hero of an S. N. Behrman short story about the middle-class aspirations of immigrant Jews, revered beautiful clothing, too. The president of a little synagogue in Worcester, Massachusetts, Mr. Wolfson is determined to look important, like a real president. Emulating the upper class, he dons a stovepipe silk hat, a Prince Albert coat, and striped trousers, an ensemble lampooned in Yiddish-speaking circles as a *prinz yankel*, to wear to Sabbath services. "The fabulous circumstance," writes Behrman knowingly, is that Mr. Wolfson "owned these garments outright. In this, he was unique in our community, such garments were nearly always hired, and seldom used except for weddings."

O. O. McIntyre, syndicated columnist and man-about-town, couldn't have been more unlike Mr. Wolfson. Yet he shared Wolfson's affinity for clothing. "I really *enjoy* snappy clothes," McIntyre acknowledged. "I have a good time selecting them. They serve in a measure to increase my sense of well-being." Good clothes had done a lot, too, for the once struggling but now prosperous salesman who wrote in the pages of the *American Magazine* of his "sartorial metamorphosis." Chronicling his conversion to clothes, the salesman described how at one point in his life he disapproved mightily of men who paid attention to their attire. " 'Spends everything he makes on himself,' " he'd sniff. Gradually, however, it dawned on him that his attitude was benighted: being better dressed and better groomed might bring him the kinds of rewards that had

A Prince Albert coat was worn on formal occasions.

hitherto eluded him. Having seen the light, he purchased a fashionable wardrobe. "In my new clothes I not only felt a different man, I *was* a different man," he confessed. "And I was treated as such."

Ready-to-wear placed gentlemanliness within the reach of men who once inhabited the outer reaches of society, enabling them to subscribe to its tenets and tout its virtues. Scrupulously honoring the "ten commandments of correct dress," salesmen, journalists, and synagogue presidents now placed a premium on uniformity and under-

Photographs taught aspiring gentlemen how to dress.

statement, sobriety and restraint. They understood that proper gents made sure their clothes "retreated" rather than "obtruded" and that their hats and shoes harmonized rather than clashed. The true gentleman dressed "cheerfully but soberly," avoided "unruly" neckties, and always wore a spotless white shirt, the "badge of the man who knows what to say when the waiter speaks to him in French." The linguistically proficient American gentleman also avoided anything that smacked of conspicuousness, such as the "luridly colored" shirts, loud checks, and gaudy waistcoats fancied by the members of the fast set. Determined not to give "offense" or, for that matter, to look like a swell, he stayed within the bounds of the perenially "correct dress chart," avoiding that which seemed

Correct Dress Chart for Winter, 1909

DAY DRESS

Coat and Overcoat	Waistcoat	Trousers	Hat	Shirt and Cuffs	Collar	Cravat	Gloves	Boots	Jewelry
Frock Chesterfield or Paletot Overcoat	White Linen Duck or White Silk	Striped Worsted or Cheviot of Dark Gray	High Silk with Broad Felt Band	Plain White with Cuffs Attached	Poke or Lap-Front	White or Pearl Ascot or Once-Over to Match Gloves	White Kid or Gray Glacé to Match Cravat	Patent Leather or Varnished Calfskin Buttoned Cloth or Kid Tops	Gold Links Gold Studs Cravat Pin
Jacket or Walking Coat Chesterfield Overcoat	To Match Coat or of Fancy Material	If with S. B. Coat, to Match If with D. B. Coat, of Same or Different Material	Derby or Alpine	Stiff or Plaited Colored with Cuffs Attached	Fold or Wing	Four-in-Hand Tie or Once-Over	Tan Cape or Reindeer	Buttoned Calf High Laced Calf or Russet High or Low	Gold Links Gold Studs
Norfolk or Double-Breasted Jacket and Overcoat	Fancy Flannel with Flap Pockets or Knitted	Tweed or Flannel	Tweed Cap or Alpine	Flannel with Soft Cuffs	Fold Deep-Point or Self-Attached Collar	Tie Neckerchief or Four-in-Hand	Chamois or Knitted	Laced Calf or Russet High or Low	Links Leather Watch-Guard
Frock or Morning Coat Chesterfield Overcoat	Double or S. B. Same Material as Coat or of White Linen Duck	Striped Worsted Light or Dark	High silk With Broad Felt Band	Plain or Piqué White with Cuffs Attached	Fold or Wing	Once-Over or Four-in-Hand	Gray Suède or Gray Reindeer	Patent Leather or Varnished Calfskin Buttoned Cloth or Kid Tops	Gold Links Gold Studs Cravat Pin

EVENING DRESS

Coat and Overcoat	Waistcoat	Trousers	Hat	Shirt and Cuffs	Collar	Cravat	Gloves	Boots	Jewelry
Cape Swallowtail Paletot or Chesterfield Overcoat	White Single-Breasted of Linen Drill Piqué or Silk	Same Material as Coat Broad Braid on Outer Seams	High Silk with Broad Felt Band Opera at Theatre	Plain or Piqué White with Cuffs Attached	Poke Lap-Front or Round-Tabbed Wing	White Tie of Plain or Figured Linen or Silk	White Glacé with Self Backs or White Reindeer White Cape for Theatre	Patent Leather or Varnished Calfskin Buttoned Cloth or Kid Tops Patent Leather Pumps	Pearl Agate or Moonstone Links and Studs
Jacket Black or Oxford Covert or Chesterfield Overcoat	Black or Gray Linen or Silk Single-Breasted	Same Material as Jacket with Plain Outer Seams	Felt or Silk-Covered Derby or Alpine	Plain or Plaited White with Cuffs Attached	Fold or Wing	Broad End Black or Gray Silk Tie	Gray Suède or Gray Reindeer	Patent Leather or Varnished Calfskin Buttoned Tops or Gun-metal Pumps	Gold Amethyst or Opal Links and Studs

Dress charts left little room for error or improvisation.

too fashionable. "What man in his senses wants to look like a fashion plate?" Correctness was far more important.

Neatness was another prerequisite of gentlemanliness, or so its guardians insisted. The American gentleman took good care of his clothes, making sure not to fling them on the nearest chair upon retiring for the evening but to put them away neatly, using wooden hangers and other modern "contrivances for keeping trousers in order." Ridding his pockets of its bulky contents—of keys, hankies, pipe and pouch, matches, and scraps of paper—lest they stretch his jackets and overcoats out of shape, the well-dressed man put on a fresh pair of celluloid shirt cuffs and collars as often as he changed his underwear, preferably once a day. And he made sure his clothes "rested." The way to prevent one's trousers from getting baggy, advised those knowledgeable about such matters, was to have at least seven different pairs: "a pair of trousers should have six days' rest to one day's work."

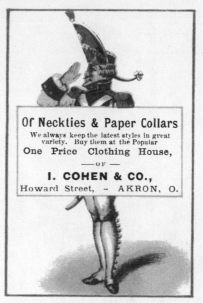

Of Neckties & Paper Collars
We always keep the latest styles in great variety. Buy them at the Popular
One Price Clothing House,
—OF—
I. COHEN & CO.,
Howard Street, - AKRON, O.

Paper collars were both disposable and affordable.

It was not enough for a pair of trousers to be well-rested, they had to be sharply creased as well. "Some years ago," reported the pseudonymous "Major of To-day," author of *Clothes and the Man* (1900), "no respectable man would dream of wearing trousers with that crease in them. Why? Because the crease was then the hallmark of the ready-made pair of trousers." But times had changed: "The man whose trousers haven't got one is considered almost slovenly." Men were very particular about their creases, confirmed the proprietor of a cleaning establishment. "A man wants the crease down his trouser leg in

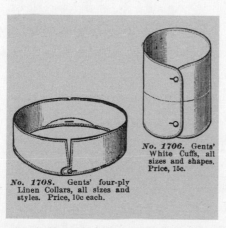

No. 1708. Gents' four-ply Linen Collars, all sizes and styles. Price, 10c each.

No. 1706. Gents' White Cuffs, all sizes and shapes. Price, 15c.

Detachable linen cuffs and collars extended the life of men's shirts.

Many African American men took great pains with their appearance.

perfect alignment between the inside and the outside seam. He wants it with a razor-like edge and he wants it to last forever!"

Men in search of social acceptance were especially alive to the aesthetics of gentlemanliness. Within the African American community, for instance, dress was a source of both individual and collective pride, an affirmation of dignity. In the wake of Emancipation, black leaders put their faith in the "gospel of civility," in "Chesterfieldian manners" and restrained dress, trusting that a show of fidelity to the strictures of respectability would confer equality or, at the very least, some degree of parity. Do not "abate, by jot or tittle, your constant endeavor to become and to be gentlemen," counseled Mrs. M. F. Armstrong, author of *Habits and Manners* (1888), a text designed for the students of Virginia's Hampton Normal and Agricultural Institute, urging the men especially to avoid "looking like a dude." At a time when the "penumbra of slavery" still clung to young black men and women, it was important to take great pains with one's appearance, she wrote, holding out the promise that "propriety of deportment on your part will do more than anything else toward securing for you fair and proper treatment from others." A decade later, E. M. Woods sounded a similar refrain in *The Negro in Etiquette: A Novelty*

(1899). Gentlemanly behavior had a lot to do with "raising the social and moral standard of the Negro," he wrote. Careful to distinguish among the "foppish fellow . . . overnice about his dress," the ne'er-do-well, and the true gent, his guidebook offered the following pointers: "Boys, don't wear your hats too high nor too low on the forehead, for it savors of the ruffian"; always wear a clean collar; don't oil your hair; and, by all means, avoid "saturating your clothing" with cologne. After all, Woods declared, turning to a higher authority for support, "what did Father Adam and Mother Eve know about cologne?"

Many African American men acted on the advice outlined in these guidebooks and took the promise of gentlemanliness to heart, especially on the Lord's Day. Every Sunday, recalled Kathleen Adams, who grew up in Atlanta during the early 1900s, all the men she knew, from her father to the local storekeepers, outfitted themselves in Prince Albert coats, striped britches, Stetson hats, walking canes, and, come winter, nice gloves. Jelly Rolly Morton remembered everyone in his crowd in New Orleans aspiring to own "at least one Sunday suit, because, without that Sunday suit, you didn't have anything." Like their city cousins, the church-going men of rural Clairborne County, Mississippi, delighted in their "good, well cared for suits and nice ties and shirts and hats." Some African American men, however, rejected the aesthetic of gentlemanliness and all that it represented. Thumbing their noses at the pretensions of polite white society, they deliberately cut flashy figures in loud suspenders, sharp shoes, brightly colored shirts and scarfs. To them, flashiness spoke of freedom while restraint spoke of repression. Within the African American community, then, clothing alternately proclaimed one's fidelity to or estrangement from middle-class America.

Immigrants also made much of what they wore. Eager to become American, they quickly learned their way around the haberdasher's, prompting journalist Hutchins Hapgood to observe at

Immigrant Jewish men proudly posed for the camera in their
stylish American clothes.

the turn of the century that immigrant Jewish men had a "keen
eye for the right thing in neckties." Others had a keen eye for
brightly colored socks and the very latest in collars, from the
"standup" model to the "high turndown." According to the *New
York Tribune*, the Lower East Side boasted many new arrivals who
worked the field of fashion with great energy. With its "sports"
(men known for their extravagantly colored socks and ties) and

"stiffs" (men known by their collars), immigrant Jewish men clearly did not lack for "artistic taste." Some among them, like the eponymous protagonist of Abraham Cahan's 1917 classic, *The Rise of David Levinsky*, sought to dress more somberly, like a "genteel American." With practice and time, he would eventually get it right, Levinsky assures himself, confident that the "difference between taste and vulgar ostentation was coming slowly, but surely." Fancying himself a gentleman, the immigrant had reason to feel that America was within his grasp: in a country where even the "poorest devil wore a hat and a starched collar," anything was possible. For one newcomer, in fact, nothing better symbolized the wonders of America than his "several suits, many shirts, his patent leather shoes and two or three kinds of hats"; such sentiments come up time and again in accounts of the immigrant experience. Even youngsters, the children of immigrants, were not immune to clothing's allure. In his memoir of growing up, music critic Samuel Chotzinoff, for instance, vividly remembers how "all manner of boys' clothing, including ravishing sailor suits with whistles attached and smart brown knee-length garbardine overcoats," gaily beckoned to him behind the plate-glass windows of local stores, where grown-up clothes were also arrayed "in all their chic and splendor on marvelous, life-sized dummies."

Real-life men, starched, pressed, and neatly encased in suit and somber tie, were ready to take on the world. Not that anyone noticed. In 1909, fifty women were interviewed by *Good Housekeeping* on the subject "His Clothes—As Seen by Her." Everyone agreed that men's clothes were not terribly interesting. When all was said and done, they told the magazine, "we have to love a man in spite of his clothes."

By the mid-1920s, this was no longer true. Growing numbers of lawyers, doctors, and college students began to loosen their

WHAT A YOUNG MAN NEEDS IN HIS SPRING WARDROBE

Two button notched lapel suit in Tamarack brown

Above: double breasted suit in Dickens blue

Four Winds topcoat with Raglan sleeves in Vellum tan

YOU spend 16 hours a day in your clothes. You'll get some fun out of them if you have several changes. Wear the Tamarack brown single breasted suit on Monday; the double breasted Dickens blue suit on Tuesday; the Pewter grey suit (shown at the right) on Wednesday—then start over again. The Four Winds topcoat will take care of you every spring day. The suits are the long wearing Gordian Worsteds

The investment for the four garments is around two hundred dollars. You'll spend more than that fixing up your car or house. Aren't you more important than either?

HART SCHAFFNER & MARX

In pitching their wares, advertisements appealed directly to the
American male's proud sense of self.

collars, experiment with color, and, much to the consternation of the National Association of Retail Clothiers and Furnishers, appear publicly in "flapping" trousers. When introduced two years earlier, commented the *New York Times* in 1927, baggy pants were merely a fad; since then, they had become a habit. Inspired by the postwar era's heightened receptivity to new, looser forms of cultural expression and what, in some quarters, was seen as a revolution in manners, "jazz attire" had infiltrated the staid confines of menswear. For the first time in centuries, men were encouraged to free themselves from the "tyranny of starch" and to dress with greater playfulness—and fewer encumbrances.

The medical and scientific communities encouraged such thinking. Men were paying a price for their "senseless garb," warned some of the nation's leading science magazines, drawing on the latest physiological research in Germany, Britain, and the United States. Close-fitting garters, scientists discovered, "hampered the blood-stream"; trousers "tightly encircled the waist," cutting off circulation; and stiff collars throttled the neck, causing headaches. Promoting perspiration, "heat stasis," and sluggishness, men's clothing was also found to be needlessly heavy. A German scientist, it was widely reported, weighed the clothing of his male assistant and of his wife, only to discover that the man's shoes alone tipped the scales. Closer to home, Dr. Donald Laird of Colgate University was widely quoted as saying that while women's fashions had gotten lighter over the years, men's had remained the same. "Men are still wearing the same gross tonnage of clothes as ever," noted the scientist, adding, for good measure, that the average American male tended to wear about a tenth of his body weight in clothes "while a dog carries only about one-fiftieth of his weight in fur." Even skeptics were encouraged to look no further than their local dance hall for proof that men's clothing was not conducive to being fleet of foot. "When we inspect the clothes worn by dancing marathoners,

The "hard-boiled gentleman" represented the American masculine ideal.

do we wonder that a woman dancer will wear out two or three partners?"

As evidence of menswear's "anomalies" mounted, men were urged to take their cue from women's fashions and to dress "lightly and airily" in loose-fitting trousers and soft collars and to dispense altogether with neckties, which, some men were now prepared to concede, had "no imaginable use whatsoever." W. O. Saunders, a newspaperman from North Carolina, was among them. A staunch believer in the "gospel of lighter clothing," Saunders sauntered down Fifth Avenue one summer day in 1929 clad only in flowing silk pajamas and a jaunty straw hat. The loosely dressed Southerner was intent on instigating a revolt as far-reaching as that of America's short-skirted women by freeing men from the weight of their clothing and, in turn, the shackles of gentlemanliness.

But his crusade went nowhere. Saunders had "dreamed of being photographed, arrested, persecuted, made to languish in jail for his creed," observed *Outlook* magazine. "He was merely photographed." A burning issue for women, dress reform found little support among American men. Their wives and daughters may have welcomed change and entertained multiple notions of womanliness but they themselves held tight to only one way of being in the world: that of the gentleman. Dress reform for men was "unsound," explained *Outlook,* making clear why the American male should not abandon gentlemanliness in favor of some new way of dressing. "Men's clothes are well enough as they are. They are concealing, they have pockets aplenty, they are of material heavy enough to retain a press and refrain from bulging. They are, mostly, dark; therefore, they are inconspicuous and do not show spots. . . . They do not flap, wilt, look funny, or get in the way, at least not much." Those in the upper reaches of society concurred. According to a 1920s survey of the apparel worn by the three hundred best-dressed men in Palm Beach, the citadel of high society, only 1 percent had taken to wearing a soft collar; everyone else preferred to be a "slave to starch" and convention. "The whole issue of the soft collar is much broader than a mere matter of fashion and taste," columnist Heywood Broun observed. "It is an inevitable symbol. Just as woman is apt to change her whole attitude toward life when she bobs her hair, so it is with the man who turns down his collar. Once he has found stimulation in one act of rebellion, he is likely to go further." Little wonder, then, that most men held back. Being a gentleman was worth far more than physical comfort or the contemplation of change.

Though reluctant to turn down his collar, the Jazz Age man gradually embraced color, squaring it with his faith in gentlemanliness. "A parade is going by!" reported the *American Mercury* in 1928. "There's an unaccustomed flash of color in the city street . . . there begins to gleam upon the horizon a glimmer of hope for the blue-serge hero . . . making a stab at decking himself out." The "drab age" in men's apparel appeared to be coming to an end, reported the chairman of the National Fashion Committee, another industry representative. With modern chemistry making more and more colors possible, on everything from taxicabs to home products, there was every reason to believe that modern men would "gather the courage to take more color unto themselves." The marketplace seemed to bear out that prediction. By the late 1920s, purveyors of men's furnishings discovered that their brightly patterned socks and "ice-cream-colored" suits were flying off the shelves; a few years earlier, they couldn't give them away. Color first crept into accessories, then spread to sportswear. The "little trio" of socks, ties, and handkerchiefs warranted "a place of honor in modern anthropologies," declared one champion of sartorial change, applauding their "noble work in raising man" from out of the gloom of gentlemanliness. "Plumage" was in, especially for golf, a sport that soared in popularity during the 1920s. "Through the medium of sports apparel," cautiously reported Columbia University professor

Paul Nystrom, "men may again be influenced to take up the use of vivid colors such as prevailed in the eighteenth century."

If nothing else, colorful clothing stirred up a lot of conversation about the masculine soul. Much like short skirts, which touched off a fierce debate about American femininity, ice-cream-colored shirts raised questions about American masculinity. Those whose preference ran to somber blacks and gentlemanly grays dismissed their brightly colored counterparts as "peacocks" whose affection for "esthetic pastel tints" was unnatural, unmanly, and un-American. Fearful lest the new form of dressing turn out to be detrimental to moral conduct, the champions of chromatic sobriety called on their fellow citizens to return to the old ways.

The peacocks, though, had biology on their side. The "male urge to color," ringingly declared the *Saturday Evening Post*, hoping to assuage its readers' anxiety, "is biologically quite as strong in civilized man as it is among, say, golden pheasants." Since it was

In his spiffy clothes, the American gentleman exuded ease and self-assurance.

a fact of nature, there was no reason for alarm at the prospect of modern man's taking his "rightful place as the 'decorative sex.'" The faint of heart shuddered at the thought and muttered darkly about "men becoming more like women," but then, they didn't know their history. Had they paid more attention to the lessons of the past, perhaps they would have realized that in wearing "proudly patterned" sweaters and ties, men were only turning back the clock to a time when "man surpassed woman in the art of dress."

Sociology was also on the side of those men partial to pastel. "Ever since I can remember there have been individuals dissatisfied with the uninteresting colors of men's conventional clothing and brave enough to break away," a longtime fabric buyer for a menswear manufacturer informed America. Writing in the pages of the *Saturday Evening Post,* he singled out the "East European element of our population" for its bravery and fashion forwardness. With their "racial love" of colors, "these people" deserved to be credited with having whetted the nation's thirst for color, he declared, offering a strikingly essentialist perspective on the relationship between race and the hues of the rainbow. His theory went something like this: When they first arrived in the New World, Jewish immigrants dressed like everyone else. Eager to be "like Americans who had been here for generations," they practiced restraint even though they found the "conventional blacks, grays and other dark shades of our male attire inherited from the Puritans dull and uninteresting." But no sooner did they become sure of themselves as Americans than they "reverted to their untrammeled love of colors," which they took with them everywhere they went, into offices, stores, and meeting places, inspiring others to follow suit. Right or wrong, the fabric buyer's theory of history underscored one of color's most important properties: its relationship to freedom.

Not surprisingly, this insider's account of how color conquered America went only so far in reassuring more traditionally minded Americans that their country was not coming apart at the seams. "Many a middle-aged man shakes his head disconsolately over this tendency to color in male apparel. He regards it as a weakening of our national fiber, a crumbling of the foundations of the republic," reported a fan of the latest trends, shaking *his* head at such misguided thinking. Men might take heart, said another, from the fact that the "tendency to color" was very much in the spirit of America. It was fueled by the need of American males, the "world's most henpecked race, to assert their independence."

A blessing or a blight, colorful men's furnishings ultimately found a place on the shelves of the nation's department stores and in the closets of men everywhere. By the late 1930s, "ventilated" fabrics had also begun to come into their own. Predicting great demand for "porosity clothes," Raymond Twyeffort, author of *Correct Fashions for Men* (1939), noted that these items weighed relatively little and were easy to wear, especially during the summer. As the palette and texture of menswear lightened, so too did attitudes about correct dress. Etiquette writers freely dispensed advice on color, helping men figure out what hues went best with what skin coloring (men with black or dark brown hair didn't have much truck with tan, it was said) and avoid "unfortunate combinations" such as

There was a young man named De Butte;
Whose knowledge of clothes was astute.
"Now rayon," he cried,
"It will be my pride,
And should make a cool summer suit!"

The first time his luck was all bad;
The suits that he bought were quite sad.
They all seemed to sag,
And hang like a bag,
Which greatly discouraged the lad.

Determined to try just once more,
He went to his favorite store.
He stated his plight
To the first clerk in sight,
Who had heard this sad story before.

Said the salesman, "You're in for a treat!
Here's a rayon that always stays neat.
Dry-cleaning, I'll state,
Won't change this fine trait.
And for coolness it cannot be beat."

At last the hard battle was won;
For now he had bought the best one.
The suit with the drape,
That will hold its shape,
Of course, is cool Airgora-Spun.

The rayon suit with the lasting shape Airgora-Spun rayon suits in attractive stripe effects, and slacks in cool pastel solid tones, are sold at America's leading stores.

SUITS $29.50 SLACKS $7.95

AIRGORA-SPUN
REG. U.S. PAT. OFF.
Luxuriously Cool
DRY CLEAN ONLY
TAILORED BY ROSE BROTHERS

ROSE BROTHERS • 275 SEVENTH AVENUE, NEW YORK 1

Synthetic fabrics like rayon revolutionized the menswear industry.

a dark blue suit with a pair of light-colored shoes. You didn't want to look like a "bag of confetti," cautioned fashion arbiter Dorothy Stote.

The boldest challenge to the ideal of gentlemanliness, though, came not from color but from jewelry. Symbols of appetite and indulgence, gold cuff links and diamond studs provoked disdain, complicating the relationship between a gentleman and his gems. According to the male-oriented "manuals of politeness" and "good form" that debuted in the years following the Civil War, the only acceptable way for a man to come directly in contact with a piece of ornamental jewelry, especially one festooned with diamonds, was to deck his wife and daughters with it. When it came to jewelry, the better part of manly valor was to wear none whatsoever: as one 1873 guidebook resoundingly put it, "the best jewel a man can wear is his honor."

Those gentlemen who wanted to sport something more tangible than their honor ran the risk of being branded as vulgar or effeminate or both. Worse still, they came perilously close to upsetting polite society, one of whose cardinal tenets held that jewelry fell squarely and exclusively within the woman's domain. From time immemorial, it was said, every woman loved jewelry. Fundamental to her femininity, this "love" was thought to be as much a part of a woman's constitution as her soft skin, silky tresses, and curvaceous breasts and hips. What, then, was America

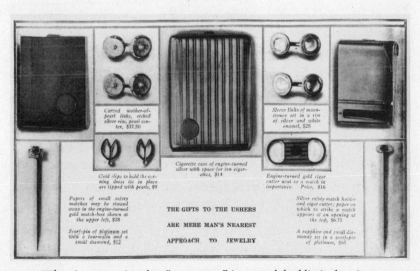

When it came to jewelry, "mere men," it seemed, had limited options.

to do with those men who shared that love? It anathematized them, placing them beyond the pale of refined society and rendering their interest in jewelry unhealthy and unmanly.

Anathema, however, was no match for reality. For one thing, a substantial traffic in men's jewelry not only existed in the 1880s and 1890s but flourished well into the interwar years. Despite the belief that "a man may go through life without possessing any valuable pieces and his friends be none the wiser," a peek into his pockets or bureau drawer told a different story: elaborately wrought gold watches and fobs, carved signet rings, perhaps a diamond stickpin or two were everywhere in evidence. Men of the Masonic persuasion possessed even more gem-studded regalia, prompting one writer for the *Saturday Evening Post* to comment wryly that obviously the wearing of bright colors and jewelry was no hardship for the thousands of men who, year in and year out, "presented themselves for initiation into the various secret orders which dress up in brilliant costumes. There would not be so many bright orange scarfs and purple socks" or, for that matter, jewelry "peeping timidly from beneath" men's waistcoats were it not so.

By the 1920s, a wide array of appropriately manly items inhabited the jeweler's showcase. There was "no lack of good attractive masculine merchandise," trumpeted the *National Jeweler* in 1925; five years later, the same magazine pointed out that "one of the traditional problems of feminine shoppers"—what to buy for their husbands, boyfriends, and fathers—had finally been alleviated, thanks to a plethora of "mannish gifts" in the marketplace. No longer was there any compulsion for jewelry-wearing men to feel awkward. Still, to be on the safe side, manufacturers made sure to highlight the appropriateness of their wares. Take, for example, that "masculine perquisite" the wristwatch, whose popularity soared in the wake of the First World War. (Cartier had pioneered its use among military men.) A man's timepiece was "as important as his tailoring in establishing his claim to correct taste," declared the makers of the Elgin wristwatch, linking their product to one of the requisites of gentlemanliness. They also went one better, harnessing it to the twin shibboleths of modernity, speed and efficiency: "An old-fashioned watch suggests an old-fashioned wearer—lagging behind the thought and method of his time. But still more important, a cumbersome design very often means lumbersome service. For in watches, as in motor cars, efficiency often increases as ugliness goes." In addition to watches, contemporary jewelers also carried "distinctly masculine" 14-karat gold belt buckles ("They grip like a bull-dog"), "sturdy" shirt studs, and handsome onyx and platinum vest buttons and matching cuff links. "Any man, every man, all men" would appreciate these things, promised their manufacturer, Krementz & Company. After all, they were "approved by Dame Fashion for their chaste designs, eminent quality and authoritative correctness."

Little by little, correctness rather than opprobrium became the "jewelry password" among men. Still, there were limits to how far they might go. "Whatever the tempting glow of gem-set cuff links, inlaid cigarette cases or gleaming rings, the man of refinement eschews them," warned one etiquette manual of the 1920s. Twenty years later, Emily Post assailed the wearing of diamonds. "Nothing is more vulgar than a display of 'ice' on a man's shirt front, or his fingers," she fumed. That being said, there was no denying that American men had taken to calling a modest amount of jewelry their own. They could still be true to themselves and wear an honest-to-goodness piece of jewelry without compromising the good name of their sturdy sex or its underpinning, gentlemanliness.

Unusually elastic, that concept endured in modern America. Where variations in women's attire yielded an altered ideal of womanliness, variations in menswear had no such effect on the corresponding ideal of gentlemanliness. Glinting jewelry, colored shirts, socks, and ties, even baggy trousers did little to dislodge the

ON BEING A DIPLOMAT AS DIPLOMA TIME APPROACHES

PUBLISHED IN THE HOPE THAT AN ELGIN WATCH COMMEMORATES YOUR GRADUATION

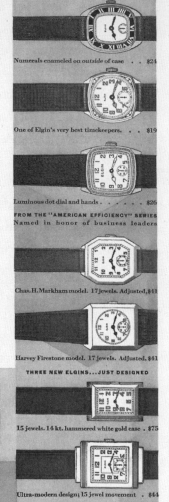

Naturally, you can't just march up to that mother or father of yours and say in so many words that you'd like an Elgin watch for graduation.

But would you mind our suggesting it?

That's what these pages are for . . . just to remind the busy race of parents of an obvious fact that might have otherwise escaped them. Now, of course, they might not see this display, there's always the chance of that. But, of course, you might see to it that they don't miss seeing it . . . That's where being a diplomat comes in.

If ever you've thought of an Elgin for your graduation present (and who hasn't?) you'll be more eager than ever now. For never have there been so many exquisite Elgins. Never has the mechanism of a watch been cased with such beauty and variety. Somewhere in this array of watches . . . the largest in the world, foreign or American, is precisely the watch to carry the sentiment of your graduation day into the years to come. For the name Elgin is still, as always, the watchword of the watch world. Near you is an Elgin jeweler ready with your graduation present. Prices range from $19 to $350.

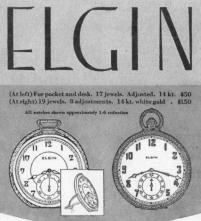

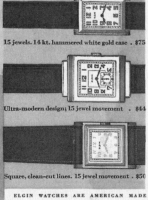

The "American efficiency" and "square, clean" look of Elgin watches
made them the ideal graduation gift, especially for men.

gentleman from his pedestal. Sustaining a few gentle knocks, he simply expanded his wardrobe to make room for a handful of novelties—and then went about his business, his integrity intact. In the meantime, most men still had to be told not to throw their clothes on a chair or "snarl" their ties in a drawer like a "nest of snakes." But even the most careless among them was now ready to admit publicly that he and his buddies cared about how they looked. "It isn't only women who like clothes," conceded the blue-serge hero at long last. "Men like them, too."

Hats provided the finishing touch.

CHAPTER FOUR

Where Did You Get That Hat?

As far as Gordon A. O'Neill was concerned, a hat was not merely "something to tip." A hat was the single most important item in a man's wardrobe, a key to his personality. "You can tell more about a man's habits and tastes by the hat he wears than by any other article of clothing," asserted O'Neill, the chief hat buyer for Lord & Taylor's Man's Shop. A man's suits offered little by way of variation, his shoes were selected for their durability, and his wife bought his ties. "But his hat is his own choice. He picks it out himself." Women, too, set much store by their hats. A cheerful model, it was said, lifted the spirits, a bedraggled one caused them to fall. "As every woman knows," said one in the know, "hats have a subtle emotional dimension: a jaunty little piece of felt with a ribbon just so can mean more to a woman's serenity or her bright self-assurance than any man will ever know." Nothing in the world, not even a bequest from a long-lost uncle, had the same "blithesome effect" on her soul as a brand-new chapeau. Seemingly a small thing, a hat bore considerable weight. A highly touted form of personal expression, it was also one of the few things Americans had in common: well into the postwar era, no adult, male or female, black or white, Christian or Jew, stepped out in public without some form of head covering. Underscoring the primacy of rules and the power of consensus in modern America, hats affirmed the relationship between the individual and the civic square.

O'Neill made sure of it. Under his watchful eye and those of his counterparts in department stores and men's shops throughout the country, the respectable male accumulated anywhere from five to twelve hats in his closet. "Fewer than five," remarked one authority, "marks a man as less than a gentleman." Elegant top hats, rakish caps, durable felt fedoras, and dapper straw boaters with the "swank of a Rajah and the ease of an old acquaintance" accommodated a wide variety of tastes and pocketbooks, as did the derby, one of the most popular styles of all. Upright and upstanding, the derby, declared the *New York Times,* was the "true headgear of democracy. Almost any man derives an air of respectability from a decently brushed derby." And it was eminently practical, to boot. Adaptable enough to see men through most social occasions, the derby stood up to rain, snow, sleet, and wind as well. It was ready to

Hat shops were once as numerous as candy stores.

"laugh at everything the weather has to offer," one derby-wearing man claimed.

For all its virtues, though, this plucky little hat wasn't easy to wear, especially if its owner was no model of masculinity. "Any man who is trim, alert and erect stands in much better chance of looking well in a derby than a man who slouches or is round-shouldered or conspicuously fat," conceded O'Neill. Such men were better off sticking to a soft felt hat or, better yet, "patronizing a gymnasium." Fans of the fedora, meanwhile, insisted the derby was bad for one's health. It "closes off the blood supply" and "increases baldness," claimed a detractor. "As a young man of 27, with ever-thinning hair, I will always cling tenaciously to a soft felt hat," said another, vowing to "holler 'De gustibus non est disputandum,' until I am bald." Even on the loftiest, fullest head of hair and a firmly muscled body, however, the homely, useful derby was "no work of art." "I wish someone would invent a new style hat for men," said an observer at the height of its prewar popularity, likening the derby to a soup bowl. *Fortune,* too, had words of ridicule. "Sometimes a man wearing a derby has suddenly seen himself in a mirror and has drawn back aghast. . . . For the first time in his life he has really *seen* a derby, has seen it *on* his head, has

A man in a derby cut a serious figure.

With a Portis straw hat perched on his head, the American male
was well protected from the elements.

caught the whole curious relation between the bulbous shape of the derby and the shape of his cranium." And yet he persisted in clamping one on his head. He felt incomplete without it.

Happily, though, relief was in sight. For those who suffered through the fall and winter months sporting a derby, spring and summer came as a welcome opportunity to don an easygoing straw or a pliable panama. Which is precisely what millions of American men did. With a fervor that cut across region, class, and religion, American men everywhere, "as standardized as Ford cars," performed the great "American hat ritual" and planted straw hats atop their heads. "Straw hats as stiff as matzohs . . . like some kind of hard yellow flower, bloomed annually all over the city on a certain sacred date—June 1st or so," recalled Arthur Miller. Though "straw hat time" varied from city to city, depending on local meteorological conditions, it commenced sometime between the fifteenth and the thirty-first of May. "Before the 15th of May no one, except the notoriety-seeker, would publicly wear a straw hat," according to the *American Hatter*, the industry's recognized authority on manly headgear, which urged retailers to develop strategies by which to inform their clients when it was socially acceptable to "blossom forth in a nice new straw." Duly advised, the American male would take out his hat, wear it for a few months, and then promptly return it to the closet or the hatbox by mid-September, at the latest. "The ides of March held no more elements of social compulsion for ancient Rome than September 15th holds for the male population of this Western Democracy. Beware!"

Of unknown origins, this unwritten law was scrupulously observed, highlighting the degree to which fidelity to convention was characteristic of modernity. In fact, those who dared to flout what was widely considered to be a universal practice, if only in America, met with surprised and contemptuous stares. The man who continued to wear his straw hat after September 15, observed the *Times*, somewhat tongue in cheek, "may even be a Bolshevik, a communal enemy, a potential subverter of the social order." At the very least, he courted public disapproval. Though in Europe a man wearing whatever hat he pleased might go about "unremarked and unmolested, well into the Autumn," remarked one disgruntled male, taboos held firm in America, where the sight of a straw hat in September was as much fair game as silk hats were to a "small boy with snowballs." Nearly a quarter of a century after visiting Philadelphia in late September, a British tourist vividly recalled his first encounter with the ritual of setting straw hats aside on a fixed date. During a sudden hot spell in late September 1899, the visitor, discomfited by the heat, asked the hotel clerk where he might purchase a straw hat. In no uncertain terms, the clerk informed him that (a) nobody, but nobody, in the City of

Hats provided a context for male fellowship and camaraderie.

Brotherly Love wore a straw hat at the end of September and (b) to venture outside with one so late in the season was to court danger. "Whether such dire results would have followed my appearance clad in the tabooed article of clothing I cannot say," the visitor recounted. Nevertheless, he decided to wear his derby instead.

Unwritten laws prescribing when a man was to take off his hat and when to keep it on were also strictly honored and carefully maintained. No gentleman would ever wear a hat in a school, theater, concert hall, private office, auction room, gallery, church, or library. To keep one on in such venues was a serious offense, a sign of disrespect that placed the offending citizen in the "pariah company of those malefactors who scribble in the margins of books or who mutilate magazines or who bring dogs into the building." Not to doff one's hat when women were about was almost as heinous. "In the presence of ladies, gentlemen remove their hats," said a student of American hat-wearing customs rather categorically, mapping out the numerous places, from apartment house elevators to restaurants and women's-wear shops, where such encounters were likely to take place. The gentleman also took off his hat when singing the national anthem, beholding a funeral, or—especially if he was a Roman Catholic or a High Church Episcopalian—passing a church of his denomination. "The increasing fondness of other sects for gothic architecture" and the general American tendency not to label churches, wryly observed the British magazine *Notes and Queries* in 1927, meant that Roman Catholics and Episcopalians often confused each other's houses of worship.

No such confusion existed between the male worshipers in a traditional synagogue and their more liberal cousins, Reform Jews. Traditionalists made sure to keep their heads covered, either with a "useful European" (i.e., Western-style) hat or with a yarmulke. Observant Jews, accustomed since the Middle Ages to covering the head while in prayer or at study, regarded the practice as sacrosanct: a time-honored way of showing respect to God, it had also come to be a symbol of Jewishness, a "feature of uniqueness" to be prized and affirmed. Either way, a covered head, traditionally minded Jews believed, was of enormous psychological importance. Reform Jews believed otherwise and, instituting a Jewish version of dress reform, dispensed with distinctive ritual attire like the yarmulke and tallis, or prayer shawl. Placing more of a premium on modern-day notions of gentlemanliness than on biblical or Talmudic precedent, they claimed that wearing a yarmulke had little to do with Jewish tradition. Rather, it was merely a custom that varied over time and place, depending on prevailing notions of decorousness. In the East, where Jews had lived for centuries, respect took the form of covering one's head, but in the West, which a majority of Jews now called home, a bare head was far more respectful. "In our time and in our land, it is the very best of manners to express respect by *un*covering the head," explained the Central Conference of American Rabbis, insisting that "hatlessness" ought to be standard American Jewish practice.

The debate created considerable tension within the American Jewish community, dramatizing the growing rift between the seemingly enduring claims of tradition and the exigent pressures—and counterclaims—of the present. By placing manners rather than religious tradition at the center of things, the hat question not only challenged the community's long-standing fidelity to distinctive sartorial norms but compelled its members to take a stand—to ally themselves completely with the modern world and its rules or to set themselves apart. Institutionalized friction was the result. To those in the Reform camp, the traditionalists' insistence on retaining the yarmulke was an "act of willful and useless self-isolation." Traditionalists returned the compliment, labeling bareheadedness an "abomination ne plus ultra" and a capitulation to secular mores. Despite pleas from moderates (especially in the Reform movement) not to let things get out of hand, the issue rankled.

Invariably, the battle also gave rise to confusion in the ranks. Writer Ruth Gay recalls the sartorially charged moment when her Yiddish-speaking father-in-law and several of his friends, dressed for the Sabbath in dark suits and hats, paid a visit to New York's Temple Emanu-El, the nation's preeminent Reform congregation. No sooner had they taken their places in the sanctuary and opened their prayer books than a congregation official appeared and said peremptorily, "Here we take off our hats in the sanctuary." The visitors, writes Gay, were astonished. "They remonstrated. They cited Talmudic law. They cited custom," but the official stood his ground. "He was master in his house and insisted that they comply with the rules." At the very last moment, though, he had a slight change of heart. Pointing to the one man among them who looked most like a traditional, old-fashioned Jew—he had a beard—the official softened his stance. "All right," he said. "This one, he can wear his hat." When seen as a symbol of the old order (even when it wasn't), a hat made sense.

In the sanctuary or on the street, hats and the variety of rules

Hats separated the men from the women.

The more fanciful the hat, the more women found it appealing.

that governed their use—when to plant one firmly on the head and when to take it off, when to wear a derby, a panama, or a yarmulke—rendered civility tangible. A display of good form and manners, wearing a hat acknowledged the power of the commonweal.

When it came to their hats, women had much greater latitude than their menfolk. Stretching and, at times, testing the limits of accountability, women were able to put all kinds of things atop their heads: "pinnacles, pokes, turrets, inverted baskets—peach or otherwise—and fabrications." Told these were hats, men were "humbly compelled to believe them," wrote one bewildered husband in 1909. From the oversize and overwrought to the saucy and the coquettish, hats tickled the female imagination. Where derbies and straw hats spoke of respectability, the creations fancied by the women of prewar America exuded flamboyance and whimsy. Many women showed "their decorative ideas first upon their heads," explained an observer, suggesting that among the fairer sex, a hat was essentially an exercise in "aesthetic development." When a poet found himself inspired, he wrote poetry. When a woman felt the same kind of "kindling sensation," she bought a hat.

Inspiration, though, was only half the story. A vital part of a woman's wardrobe, a hat was deemed such an essential and unquestioned attribute of femininity that it alone could make or unmake a woman's appearance. Since "much of the smartness of your costume depends on your hat," women were told, they should attempt to "give it *great* consideration and to be sure that it is right for you in every particular." Living up to such standards was by no means easy; even the most resolute of authorities conceded that. But if every woman made certain to take her time and to "wield a hand mirror" before settling on a confection of feathers, lace, and flowers, she was, they believed, far less likely to make a mistake. "A hat may be very becoming in front and exceedingly grotesque in profile," counseled a columnist in the *American Jewess,* urging female readers to look at themselves from every angle when choosing one. Another sartorial authority, a self-styled "Fifth Avenue costumer," urged simplicity on his customers, especially those who tended to be somewhat overweight. If a stout customer stubbornly elected to disregard his advice and demanded all manner of flowers and ribbons on her hat, he put a special mark on her sales slip. It reminded him that "any complaint is on the customer's own head." Owning a number of different hats, each tailored to a specific occasion, was another way to avoid a potentially perilous situation. "If a woman must, she can manage with two," allowed one millinery expert. "She can have a very plain and simple morning hat and a dainty afternoon one. Of course," the expert hastened to add, "three hats are better: a sports, a shopping and a semi-dress one. A fourth hat would make it possible to discriminate between simple and more formal afternoon functions while 5th, 6th and so forth means a hat for every costume, which is every woman's ideal."

The growing affordability of hats made such advice possible. By the 1910s, the "standardized smart hat" took its place alongside shirtwaists, stockings, and shoes in the wardrobes of American women; stores now carried hats in every price range. Expensive, one-of-a-kind hats didn't suffer for want of an audience, either. In the years preceding and immediately following World War II, women with a highly sophisticated palate and the means to indulge it could find much to please them at the atelier of John-Fredericks or that of Lilly Daché, whose creations, it was said, were "as sure to have smartness as a Steinway is to have tone." Custom-made hats like theirs set the standard against which all others were measured: "When they tilt a brim thus and so, the news permeates the millinery business with something approaching the speed of light." While a John-Fredericks hat might set a customer back $28.50 and a Daché creation upward of $20.50, smartly styled copies were available for as little as $5.00 or even $1.95. And women bought in droves: hats with provocative brims and a surfeit of feathers and hats without; cloches, turbans, berets, and boaters.

Mindful of the hat's importance—for some, it was said to be a "life-or-death interest" while others described it as a "necessity of life, like food"—the American woman of the prewar era rarely ventured outside without one. She wore one to work and to market, to meetings and afternoon tea, on the street and, especially, at worship, prompting the *New York Times* to observe that women in their special Sunday hats seemed "so much prettier in church than anywhere else." Many women, like Miss Higgins, the organist at a Presbyterian church in one small American town, reserved their best and most elaborately trimmed creations for church. Though it was not easy to find the right balance between "personal preference and something befitting the solemnity of Divine Service," Miss Higgins's hat struck just the right note. "Pyramids of grapes and flowers, clusters of yellow wheat and curving shafts of aigrettes undulated and swayed to the bobbing rhythms" of the familiar church hymns, recalled one entranced eyewitness, noting with particular relish how the feathers on the organist's hat seemed to come to life and lead the congregation in prayer.

Hats also enlivened the churchgoing experience of African American women, who, like Miss Higgins, took much pleasure in the swooping brims and formidable crowns of their "Sunday-go-to-church hats." Bedecked with ribbons, feathers, or rhinestones, depending on what was fashionable, these creations pleased the eye, elevated the spirit, and conferred respectability and dignity on African American churchgoers, for whom Sunday was a "day of dress" as well as a day of rest. The church, after all, was one of the few places where African American women could escape the constrictions of the workaday world, a place where they could exchange their starchy maid's outfits for stylish ensembles that, from head to toe, reflected their individuality. "Work clothes—nondescript and uniform—tended to erase the black body," explain Shane White and Graham White in their study of the expressive culture of

The Women's Committee of Brooklyn's First AME Zion Church attended meetings as well as religious services suitably behatted.

Two unidentified South Carolina women of the 1920s put on their very best hats
to have their picture taken by photographer Richard Samuel Roberts.

African Americans. "Sunday clothing enhanced and proclaimed it." A show of good manners, a mark of respect to those in the pews and those on high, "wearing a hat in God's house" doubled as a form of insurance. "God is awfully busy on Sunday mornings," a Washington church elder pointed out. "I just want to make sure I'm wearing something that might catch His eye."

Setting their sights a bit lower, immigrant women also fancied ornately ornamented hats. "Does Broadway wear a feather? Grand Street dons two," related the *New York Tribune* at the turn of the century, referring to the celebrated Lower East Side thoroughfare on which America's newest citizens, outfitted in the latest millinery concoctions, shopped and strolled. "The average East Side girl," the paper continued, "buys a new hat every winter, preferably one with feathers. It is always a large one, and sometimes it groans beneath the weight of nearly or quite a dozen plumes which may once have called an ostrich their parent." Young immigrant women and their mothers took pleasure in wearing an extravagantly plumed hat, delighting in themselves and in America. In the Old Country, where modesty and propriety went hand in hand, married women routinely covered their heads with a kerchief or a wig (*sheitel*); some women wore both. In America, though, things were different: women were free to play by a new set of rules. Encouraged by Yiddish women's magazines as well as by their neighbors to discard their "old-fashioned" head coverings—they were "unhealthy, unlovely and unaesthetic," editorialized one magazine—married immigrant women substituted a "rakish" hat instead. In the process, the covered head was transformed from a traditional symbol of modesty into an affirmation of American-ness, leading Rabbi Moses Weinberger to estimate at the turn of the century that in the New World "only two in a thousand" women covered their heads for religious reasons. "Most Jews have all but forgotten that there are any regulations regarding this matter at all," he glumly concluded.

For Paulina, Anna, and Gitel Forman, the elaborately trimmed hat
symbolized America.

Hadassah luncheons provided an opportunity for members to wear their finest chapeaux.

Others, however, regarded the change with greater equanimity, seeing in it a symbol of America's possibilities. "The girl whose Russian mother knew but the wig of the religious Jewess and a soft shawl, the girl who, had she remained in bright Italy, would have kept one kerchief for weekdays and another for Sunday—these girls feel vastly fine in a 'three-story hat' which might well vie with the historic coat of Joseph," noted one of Weinberger's contemporaries, invoking a biblical reference to legitimate contemporary American notions of style. "In the land of equality shall not one wear what another wears?"

At no time was this imperative more keenly felt than on holidays, a time for "eye-smiting display." "Prepare for Easter! Hail to the Lily! Welcome Spring!" trumpeted the *Illustrated Milliner*, a monthly whose "cheerful" and "sprightly" treatment of millinery matters squarely linked the rituals of Easter to those of fashion. "Whatever critics may say of the custom of donning new raiment at Easter time, it seems a pretty fashion, grounded in good taste," the magazine explained in 1900. "To do honor to one of the most joyous festivals of the Christian year, by acknowledging it with brighter apparel, when possible, is good for everyone." Thousands upon thousands of churchgoers throughout the nation seemed to agree. Putting their stamp of approval on the practice, they transformed the street as well as the sanctuary into a spectacle, a "matchless exhibition of new gowns, Spring wraps and modish millinery."

The Easter parade became one of America's most cherished institutions, a symbol of its plenitude as well as its piety. "To see and be seen [is] the prime object" of the day, noted one spectator who, together with a hundred thousand other celebrants, spent his Easter Sunday strolling along Atlantic City's fabled boardwalk. The event, he gushed, was "to the United States what the Grand Prix is to Paris." Elsewhere throughout the nation, the Easter parade made front-page news by elevating the humble hat to an object of communion. As the *Ladies' Home Journal* put it more prosaically, it was "easy to greet the Easter morn with smiles when one own[ed] a saucy little" hat.

Jewish women felt the same impulse when, a few months later, Rosh Hashanah, the Jewish New Year, rolled around. "*This* is the time to select a New Hat," advised the *Connecticut Hebrew Record* in September 1920, encouraging Jewish women to time their millinery purchases to coincide with the fall festival, which, of course, many did. Appearing in synagogue in a brand-new hat became as much a part of the Jewish New Year celebration as the distinctive prayer service or the eating of apples and honey cake. In American Jewish homes, as well as in Christian ones, then, a new holiday hat provided a lift, heightening a personal as well as a communal sense of renewal—a feeling duly acknowledged, and

FIGURE No. 6.—LADIES' WALKING HAT.

FIGURE No. 7.—LADIES' SAILOR HAT.

FIGURE No. 1.—LADIES' TURBAN.

FIGURE No. 8.—LADIES' LEGHORN HAT.

FIGURE No. 2.—LADIES' CARRIAGE HAT.

FIGURE No. 9.—LADIES' HAT.

FIGURE No. 3.—LADIES' HAT.

FIGURE No. 10.—LADIES' BONNET.

FIGURE No. 4.—LADIES' HAT.

FIGURE No. 11.—LADIES' LEGHORN HAT.

HATS AND BONNETS.
(For Descriptions See Pages 672 and 673.)

FIGURE No. 5.—LADIES' TRIMMED SAILOR-HAT.

Festooned with ribbons, flowers, or feathers, women's hats dazzled the eye.

gently mocked, by the *Illustrated Milliner* in a poem entitled "The Reason Why":

Devout she sits within her pew
A vision fair, with eyes of blue
A face divine, serenely sweet
In calm repose, content complete;
Her thoughts must dwell above the skies
Within the pale of Paradise.

The mighty music fills her soul
And through the church its echoes roll;
Amid the throng that worships there
She sits, devout in peace and prayer
And perfect bliss— for, though you search,
She has the finest hat in church.

Not all churchgoers, though, were quite as understanding or sympathetic as the *Illustrated Milliner*. Clergymen from John Wesley in the eighteenth century to Boston's Cardinal O'Connell in the twentieth had a particularly long history of making snide comments about the hats worn by their female congregants. Wesley repeatedly ranted against the "elephantine" hats of his female followers, describing them as "scandals in female modesty." O'Connell picked up where Wesley left off. "You can tell the quality of a woman's brain by the kind of hat that covers it," he said dismissively. As hats grew larger and much more ornate—between 1908 and 1910, for instance, they typically measured three feet tall and two feet wide and sported "dangerous pins, and stiff, sharp, pointed feathers" or "heaps of flowers"—clerical disdain grew even more pronounced. Ever since the early days of the church, women's hats have been a subject of eccleciastic concern, "but never has the subject been so vital and vexing as during the last year," insisted the Reverend Charles E. Jefferson, pastor of New York's Broadway Tabernacle Church, in 1909. "This is because the style of bonnet or hat has been abnormally immense and the discomfiture of the worshippers . . . has been correspondingly great. *What to do with the women* has been a problem in churches throughout the country." Even Saint Paul himself wouldn't have known what to do, added the *Times,* referring to the man responsible in the first place for insisting that Christian women cover their heads while at prayer. "Fancy that outspoken Apostle looking down from a platform on a sea of such hats as the Spring of 1910 is producing!"

Paul's heirs, however, knew exactly what to do. Some clergymen boldly suggested that those female congregants inclined to fashionably excessive hats sit at the back of the church or, better yet, leave their hats at home. Father Thomas J. O'Brien, a Roman Catholic priest, recommended wearing a shawl, as Italian churchgoing women did: "Besides showing a more meek Christian spirit, there is less danger in this style of sticking feathers or daggers in the eyes of the men." Others recommended that their female congregants don a demure and unadorned hat —a church hat, they called it—or else contemplate the prospect of sitting bareheaded, as was the custom at the theater or the opera. Still others, like the pastor of the First Baptist Church in Somerville, Massachusetts, proposed that women who insisted on wearing "fancy millinery" be barred from services altogether, an idea that quickly spread from New England to Pennsylvania, where a coalition of ministers in Pittsburgh "declared war" on big hats.

Such strident rhetoric made it clear that the clergy saw the big hat not as just another of life's petty irritations but as a major problem, one that placed whimsy at odds with responsibility and the rights of the individual against the needs of the community. From where they sat, everything about the big hat spelled trouble.

A pretty hat was heaven.

For starters, its "length and depth and breadth and height" obstructed the congregation's view of the proceedings on the pulpit. In one instance, this actually turned out to be a godsend. One Easter Sunday in 1908, a fire broke out in St. John's Catholic Church in St. Louis: bouquets of paper lilies had gotten too close to the candles. Fortunately, though, no one panicked at the sight of flames shooting from the altar because most worshipers were unable to see a thing. The "wide spreading Easter creations" clustered at the front of the church blocked their view. "Women's vanity, which led them to sit at the front of the church where they could be seen to best advantage, probably saved scores from injury," reluctantly conceded Father J. Stepan, the church's religious leader. Most of the time, though, big hats were a safety hazard. Capable of poking out an eye or lacerating a face, they also gave rise to congestion in the pews, especially come Easter, when churches were unusually filled with worshipers. "Pews which have comfortably accommodated 6 persons would safely hold no more than 4 when all wore hats 2 or 3 feet in diameter," complained overtaxed church ushers.

And that wasn't all. Big hats like those worn at Easter simply did not belong in church, insisted the clergy. Extravagant, excessive, and expensive, they were not in keeping with the modest demeanor Christianity expected of its devotees. More disturbing still, they distracted worshipers from the business at hand, causing "women to spend more time examining hats than they do listening to the sermon" and making it difficult for their menfolk to "concentrate [their] minds on God." Women might fritter away their spiritual energies on a hat but, when all was said and done, they could still be counted on to attend religious services. With men, though, it was a different matter entirely. Their connection to organized religion was thought to be so tenuous that the smallest provocation might send them packing. "These days, we hear a lot about women's rights," fumed Brooklyn churchgoer Henry Murray Calvert in 1910. But what of men's rights? Having long and patiently borne the "vexation" of large hats, "we respectfully ask the women for the sake of blessed charity to stop it." If they didn't, he predicted darkly, men were not long for the church. For his part, the Reverend M. H. Armor of New Jersey warned his female congregants that if they continued to wear big hats in the front pews they would have to "answer for more than one man starting on the downward path."

As much a public nuisance as a churchly one, the big hat also complicated the rituals of daily life in the metropolis, forcing citizens to alter their patterns of perambulation, transportation, and leisure. A woman wearing a big hat "occupies the space of two persons on the platform and blocks ingress and egress, while she greatly increases the discomfort and, appreciably, the peril of subway travel," complained one offended New Yorker, who recommended she be charged double fare. Hatpins, the "fad of the hour," were an additional source of concern. As hats grew larger, they required a greater number of hatpins, and more elaborately styled ones at that, to keep them in place. "The hatpin is increasing in size," related one observer in 1909. "Possibly to keep pace with the picture hat," it now measured 3½ inches in diameter. "Ladies, when you are just tall enough for your hats to be on a level with the faces of men around you, keep those hats, with their dangerous steel pins, perfectly still. Thank you!" one imperiled man beseeched in a letter to the *Times*.

Urban theatergoers also complained about the "hat evil." So much so, in fact, that management explicitly declared it off-limits. Some women obligingly went bareheaded, others held their hats in their laps during the performance ("the rise of the curtain causes the well-bred to unhat," reported one theatergoer), and still others sought an alternative form of ornamentation. "There is no need of bemoaning the fact that the hat is definitely barred from the theatres, for the new coiffure ornaments decreed and ordained by Paris will more than compensate one for the sacrifice," cheerfully advised the *Illustrated Milliner*, recommending that women festoon their heads with sparkly new hair ornaments instead. "The dernier chic," it pointed out, was a tiara of gold or silver lace or a delicate Juliet cap. In the meantime, a number of theater owners considered taking their cue from some of their French counterparts, who had successfully devised a clever solution to the hat problem by dividing their theaters into two sections: women "avec chapeaux" to the right, women "sans chapeaux" to the left. In New York, the Shubert-owned theaters took a different tack, choosing to make the fashionably behatted feel welcome regardless of where they sat. "Women who wear the new big Spring hats need not be afraid to go to Daly's Theatre," declared the Shuberts reassuringly. A separate rack had been set aside to hold the hats during the show and a "regular milliner's assistant" would be on hand to assist women with them at its conclusion.

The Shuberts notwithstanding, opposition to the big hat continued. The *New York Times,* among others, proposed a radical solution: dispense with it altogether. Given the dangers it posed to both the physical and the moral health of the general population, why not retire the big hat, suggested the newspaper, which had frequently railed against it on its editorial page. Surely no one would mourn its passing. After all, the big hat was "obnoxious alike to the aesthete, the moralist and the voluptuary."

Most women, however, didn't see things quite that way. Though a few, like Abby Hedge Coryett, urged their sisters to be sensible—"Big hats are a nuisance everywhere, and it is only once in a great while that they are beautiful," she wrote to the editor of the *Times*—more women by far delighted in them. "There is nothing to take [their] place in elegance, nor in picturesqueness of outline, nor in general becomingness," they said, playing by a different, far more elastic set of rules. From their perspective, a hat did not merely decorate a woman's person, announce her social station, proclaim her fidelity to the commonweal, or get in the way. A woman's hat, from the most elaborate "floral and faunal marvel" to the flimsiest piece of tulle, spiritedly proclaimed her uniqueness. Indulging the imagination, it freed women everywhere to believe that the "right hat on the right head is poetry."

FOX

AS DAINTY AND ALLURINGLY CLEVER IN ITS FASHION NICETY AS A PINK RIBBON ON A BIT OF LINGERIE.

THERE IS SOMETHING FASCINATING ABOUT FOX FOOTERY THAT THE AVERAGE LINES OF PUMPS, SLIPPERS AND OXFORDS DO NOT HAVE AND IT IS THAT "SOMETHING" THAT PLACES FOX PRODUCTIONS IN A CLASS BY THEMSELVES.

THIS IS A POPULAR PRICED LINE BUT WITH AN EXCLUSIVENESS THAT IS USUALLY ASSOCIATED ONLY WITH THE HIGH PRICED FOOTERY.

FOX FOOTERY REPRESENTS THE LONG PROFIT FOR RETAILERS. THE NEW LINE IS ON DISPLAY AT OUR VARIOUS SALES ROOMS.

WE INVITE YOU TO SEE IT.

CHAS. K. FOX, Inc.
HAVERHILL, - - MASS.

CHICAGO: Great Northern Building.
BOSTON: 54 Lincoln Street.
NEW YORK: Marbridge Building, Broadway ⊕
34th Street, Room 632

American "footery" aroused great passion among shoppers.

CHAPTER FIVE

~

Oh, My Aching Feet!

"Men and women with unhappy feet are bound to be uncomfortable and unhappy themselves," the Holeproof Hosiery Company of Milwaukee observed early in the twentieth century, urging Americans to "forget all this unhappiness" by purchasing its brand of "antiseptic, soft and soothing sox" and stockings. By then, American-made shoes, available in as many as ten different sizes and in widths that ranged from A to E, furthered the nation's chance at happiness, especially when they, too, promised to alleviate or at least minimize pedal discomfort. "The era of Good Sense is surely here," trumpeted one trade publication in 1898, pointing with pride to the line of sensible footwear developed by James S. Coward. "Although his shoes are not especially attractive to the eye, his customers testify to their ease and hygienic qualities." In an America increasingly conscious of its health, that meant a lot. Eager to transform themselves into fleet-footed Mercurys and Dianas, Americans elevated the humble shoe to a vessel of well-being. Fashion, however, complicated matters. Tempting consumers with shiny patent leather shoes, dainty evening slippers, and snug-fitting boots, it forced them to choose between health and beauty, comfort and vanity. Whatever value they endorsed—sometimes it was health, at other moments it was beauty—modern Americans ended up paying a lot of attention to their feet.

When it came to their footwear, everyone, including Mr. Coward, agreed there was no such thing as the perfect shoe. Whether a 4½ or a 6¾, the "shoe in all its forms is, first, a necessary evil, and second, in the very nature of it, a compromise," explained Dr. Woods Hutchinson, a physician specializing in pedal maladies. "Everything that the foot gains in efficiency and in safety from boots or shoes it must pay a price, yes, a penalty." Encased and immobilized in a "leather coffin," the foot perspired, expanded, blistered, and chafed. No wonder, then, that 90 percent of Americans, according to the American Museum of Safety, suffered from foot problems. Cramped, ill-fitting, and impractical, most shoes were about as good for walking as "sardines in a tin are for swimming."

Shoe manufacturers came to the rescue in the 1890s. Harnessing health to technology, they developed the Eureka and other "extreme comfort-giving" shoes whose "arch supports," "flexible shanks," and broad, square toes conformed to the outline of the foot. Customers who purchased a pair reported that they felt instantaneous relief upon slipping them on. In no time at all, the testimony of satisfied customers able to enjoy their daily constitutional thanks to their Arch Preservers, Ground Grippers, and Good Sense shoes swelled sales of the sensible shoe. Americans also had the option of donning Persian slippers, "the most aesthetic foot-covering," or of following in the footsteps of the

The sensible shoe sought to blend good looks with good health.

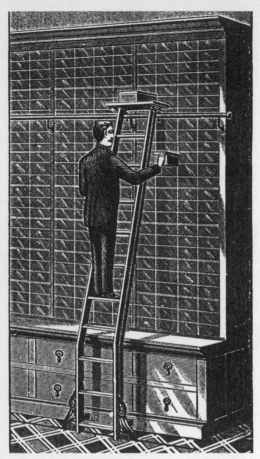
By the turn of the century, stores were filled to the rafters with different kinds of shoes.

native American Indian by sporting moccasins. Soft, pliant, easy on the soles and the toes, the leather moccasin of the "aboriginal Indian," explained dress reformer Helen Ecob, "takes precedence of our modern chausserie in its adaptation to the needs of the feet." "Our native Indians," added Dr. Charlotte C. West, "stand, walk and run with great assurance, dignity and even majesty." Now all Americans could emulate them—or at least their shoes.

Health reformers, in turn, encouraged consumers, especially female ones, to seek out the sensible shoe. Fanciful footwear, they claimed, hobbled the feminine form much like its cousin the corset. "A trim foot and a neat ankle are still feminine attributes on which a woman may pride herself and justly so; but they need not and should not be secured at the expense" of good health, reformers insisted. Surveying women's footwear, with its delicately worked leather, pointy toes, and curvy heels, they wondered if it was possible to imagine "anything more senseless, inconvenient, uncomfortable and unshapely." By their lights, the Wilhelmina and other stylishly cut models crippled the foot, crammed the toes ("Civilized beings scarcely know how important a part is played by the toes," chided one reformer), and forced women to droop, tilt, or thud when they walked. And that wasn't all. Irritability was another reported casualty of the bad shoe, inefficiency a third. "No woman can be good-natured when her feet hurt," related journalist Elizabeth Sears. "We are joined in one vast sisterhood of sympathy with the one who sighs with relief after she has painfully limped the last few blocks home and groans as she exchanges her smart, high-heeled boots for the faithful, old, downtrodden house shoes."

Smart shoes also reportedly got in the way of the American work ethic, hampering the ability of office workers to do their jobs effectively. "No girl can become an efficient typist if she wears high heels," insisted the manager of a business school for women. "It interferes with proper posture, and unless you know how to sit properly at your work you cannot give your best energy to the work before you." Risible as these claims may now seem, the perils of stylishness were not to be underestimated. High heels, grimly reported the *Ladies' Home Journal*, caused the death of 1,149 women in 1916 (unsteady on their feet, they tripped and fell) and crippled an additional 4,000, while the number of injuries to the back, spine, head, and "temper" was simply incalculable. "Nature planned our feet for use rather than ornament and nature generally makes us pay up in the long run for any transgression of her laws," it cautioned.

Newcomers to America also found it difficult to reckon with the stylish shoe—but for different reasons. Despite the popular adage that "Americanization begins at the foot," Fannie Shoock and immigrants like her were utterly confounded at first by the exaggerated contours of American footwear. Accustomed

The sturdy foot rest made the shoe salesman's job a lot easier.

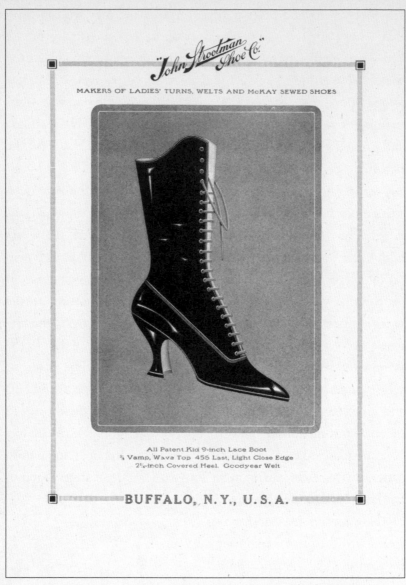

Shiny patent leather boots had a certain "something" about them.

to thick-soled, tightly laced boots meant to last year in and year out, she couldn't help wondering, "What's wrong here? What kind of country is this? People have pointy feet." Another new arrival, a Mrs. Addiego, objected not so much to pointy feet as to patent leather shoes whose reflective surface, she believed,

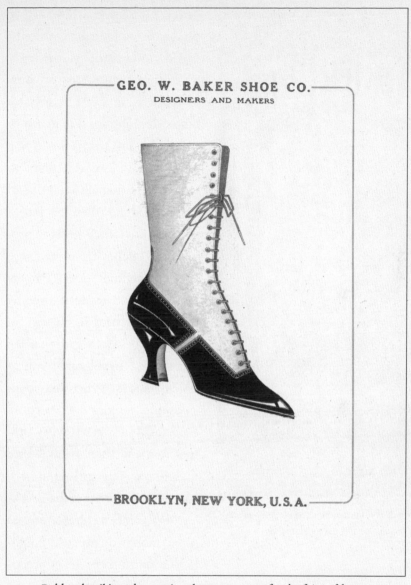

GEO. W. BAKER SHOE CO.

DESIGNERS AND MAKERS

BROOKLYN, NEW YORK, U.S.A.

Bold and striking, these pointy boots were not for the faint of heart.

revealed what it shouldn't. Far too suggestive to be acceptable, the patent leather shoe was banished from the wardrobe of her daughters and their friends. But then, patent leather wasn't just morally suspect; it also required considerable upkeep. "Nice patent-leather makes the neatest of footgear, but it requires care to keep it in

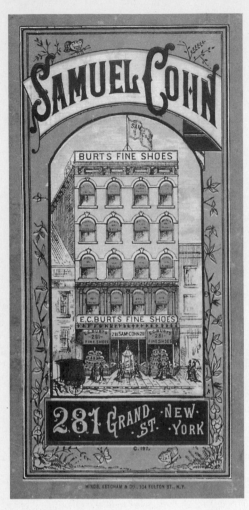

Uptown and downtown, shoe stores were a fixture of the urban economy.

order," observed a 1902 article on shoe maintenance, providing a number of surprisingly utilitarian suggestions on how to treat it right. "There is no better dressing for it than a very little salad oil. Before wearing a new pair . . . it is expedient to well rub in a small quantity of salad oil, and then to polish with a soft cloth. This is to prevent the leather from cracking, as it sometimes does. Patent-leather should never be dried by the fire, for heat has a way of causing the leather to harden and crack." In still other households, shoes generated considerable emotional friction, especially between Old World mothers and their New World daughters. The girls, reported social worker Sophonisba Breckenridge, much preferred to spend money on expensive high-heeled and otherwise impractical footwear like patent leather shoes while their mothers insisted on shoes that were not only sensible but cheaper. Unable to resolve their differences, mothers and daughters quarreled, and quarreling led to domestic distress.

Despite the manifold limitations of fashionable shoes, most consumers favored them over their sensible alternative. Women, in particular, balked at the prospect of trying on "common-sense"

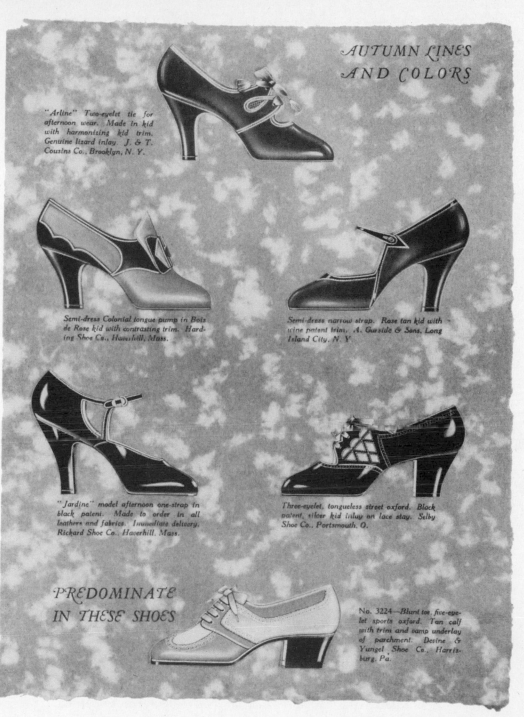

"Arline" Two-eyelet tie for
afternoon wear. Made in kid
with harmonizing kid trim.
Genuine lizard inlay. J. & T.
Cousins Co., Brooklyn, N. Y.

Semi-dress Colonial tongue pump in Bois
de Rose kid with contrasting trim. Hard-
ing Shoe Co., Haverhill, Mass.

Semi-dress narrow strap. Rose tan kid with
wine patent trim. A. Garside & Sons, Long
Island City, N. Y.

"Jardine" model afternoon one-strap in
black patent. Made to order in all
leathers and fabrics. Immediate delivery.
Richard Shoe Co., Haverhill, Mass.

Three-eyelet, tongueless street oxford. Black
patent, silver kid inlay on lace stay. Selby
Shoe Co., Portsmouth, O.

*PREDOMINATE
IN THESE SHOES*

No. 3224—Blunt toe, five-eye-
let sports oxford. Tan calf
with trim and camp underlay
of parchment. Devine &
Yungel Shoe Co., Harris-
burg, Pa.

In the 1920s, manufacturers often gave their shoes fanciful women's names.

models, and it is not hard to see why. Resembling "thumbless mittens" and "ferryboats," they were not terribly attractive. For another thing, they highlighted rather than hid the peculiarities of the foot, prompting Dr. Hutchinson, the specialist, to claim that "many of the so-called hygienic and reformed shoes are as gross a libel on the human foot . . . and as ill-fitting and absurd as the fashionable models shown in plate-glass windows." The high-heeled shoe, in contrast, made women feel taller, thinner, and lovelier. Doctors might protest and dress reformers complain, but female consumers across the country routinely chose stylish footwear. They didn't care if a shoe hurt, women were prone to say, so long as it was pretty.

In the name of some higher good, Americans might adjust their hemlines, remove their hats, and stay clear of bright-colored shirts. But when it came to their shoes, they made a clear choice between the emotional well-being associated with being fashionably shod and the physical well-being that resulted from being properly shod. And they stuck by their stylish footwear, their health be damned. Blisters, corns, and bunions were a small price to pay for stylishness, they resolved, taking only a few minutes to make up their minds. (Industry studies confirmed that men spent a mere 5 minutes deciding what to buy. It took women slightly longer—12.2 minutes on average—to arrive at a decision.) Squeezing their feet into shoes whose toes were as sharply filed as toothpicks, most Americans preferred to sacrifice themselves on the "altar of vanity."

For all the talk about the perils of fashion and the vanity of its followers, it took a war—the First World War—to focus the nation's attention on its feet. Until then, the ill-fitting shoe was commonly believed to be a consequence of femininity or, as the *Times* categorically stated in 1909, "it is a fact, attested to by the most learned sociologists, that nearly all women demand shoes several sizes smaller than their feet." The sociologists, though, had it wrong, as the army was soon to discover. Most recruits, a study conducted by the Army Shoe Board revealed, not only were completely ignorant of their shoe and sock sizes but tended, almost as a matter of course, to jam their lower extremities into shoes several sizes too small. As vain as women, they refused to heed the experts' advice and were "unwilling, without mathematical demonstration," to accept shoes of the "dimension they ought to wear." More worrisome still, the enlisted man, the army's physicians discovered, typically displayed a "universal aversion to walking." "Surrounded by mechanical contrivances of all types, he saves himself the effort and takes the path of least resistance." This type of man, they concluded, "will usually have undeveloped [and] relatively weak feet," ill-suited to military service.

The military did not take these findings lightly. Keenly aware that "a foot soldier who is impaired in his locomotion is no longer a good soldier," it advised those in command to pay as much attention to caring for the feet of their men as the "calvary officer devotes to the care of the feet of his horses." Toward that end, the armed services systematically made use of a number of newfangled instruments, from pedographs with their metal knobs and blades to Roentgen or X rays with their silvery silhouettes, to take the measure of every recruit's foot. Once the width and the length of the foot were scientifically ascertained (that is, on the basis of "fact rather than opinion"), the Resco Marine Corps Shoe-Fitting System made sure these coordinates corresponded to at least one of 138 different shoe sizes that the army kept in stock. "Shoes are properly to be regarded as much more than mere clothing," urged Major Edward Lyman Munson, author of an official handbook on the "soldier's foot and the military shoe." They were the "agent on which the mobility of the infantry depends and the accomplishment of tactical purposes is possible."

In the years that followed, alarmed civilians eagerly drew on

The U.S. armed forces took great pains to ensure that servicemen's shoes fit properly.

both the army's findings and its appliances to propagandize on behalf of sensible shoes. "Can anyone, most especially a retail shoe salesman, know these facts without being stirred, and without instantly resolving never to be a party willingly to improper, harmful shoe fitting, with its inevitable injurious results?" ringingly affirmed a spokesman for the American shoe industry in 1920. Retailers now vowed to redouble their efforts at correct shoe fitting. Scientizing salesmanship, they raised the status of the shoe salesman from clerk to professional. "True salesmanship is an effort of brains," insisted the Boston-based Retail Shoe Salesman's Institute, which in 1920 inaugurated a forty-eight-week training course in shoe fitting, shoe store management, and footwear advertising. Familiarity with the foot's anatomy, an awareness of purported racial differences ("Races differ somewhat in foot construction and consideration should be given to this fact"), and detailed knowledge of the "principles of correct shoe fitting" were what made a "true shoe salesman actually a *consulting expert*." Rising to great rhetorical heights, the institute's instructors pro-

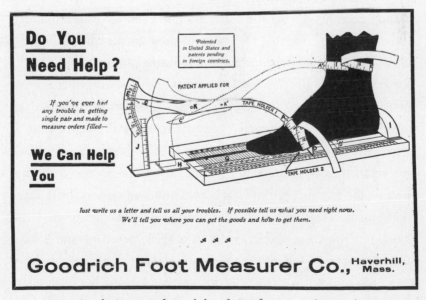

Measuring devices transformed shoe fitting from an art into a science.

nounced shoe fitting a sacred trust: "None can minimize its importance or honorably evade its responsibility. With the single exception of corset-fitting (and this is certainly in second place) no sphere of wearing apparel service to the public is so charged with moral and physical duty."

With the help of their trained shoe salesmen, more and more American women now began to sing the praises of the well-fitting, sensible shoe. "Listen to any group of women as they discuss styles," reported one popular American magazine of the twenties. "When the conversation turns to smart shoes, someone will declare that there is no use in shoe smartness unless it is combined with comfort and foot freedom; and *all* will agree." Some women had grown accustomed to the low-heeled shoe while serving as nurses, Salvation Army "lassies," and YWCA training camp personnel during the war. "Built for service rather than for looks," it complemented the uniform these women proudly wore and—for a few years, at any rate—enjoyed a certain vogue. Others were swayed by the power of X rays. For years, home economics instructors at Iowa State College had been frustrated in their attempts to persuade female students to wear the right kind of shoe. Too many girls, they complained, "like showy shoes and . . . intend to stick to them, rain or shine, advice or no advice." That despite the fact that out of nearly two hundred seniors, only three had normal feet. ("The college should graduate them 'cum laude.' ") But then two instructors, a Miss Merchant and a Miss Cranor, hit upon the idea of X-raying the bones of their students from top to bottom, confident that science would convince where moral exhortation did not. As expected, when the undergraduates saw the results they were horrified. Much as they liked to think of themselves in heels as lithe, graceful swans, X rays revealed them to be "ewe-necked and pot-bellied, twisted and curved" creatures whose pelvises tipped forward awkwardly at a forty-degree angle. Not surprisingly, the students swore off high heels at once. Like the X ray, the mirror was also pressed into service as an agent of somatic reform. "Mirrors have a reputation for being aids to vanity, but, properly used, they have an opposite effect," enthused Dr. Eleanor Bertine, director of the YWCA's Bureau of Social Education. When young women viewed themselves in a mirror (a "big triple mirror" was best), they saw themselves as never before. "Oh, those mirrors are very chastening," she exclaimed.

Still others, determined to put the country completely on "another footing," launched a national campaign designed especially for the "woman who finds herself with too much time on her hands—and ill-fitting shoes on her feet." Pronouncing shoe reform a woman's issue much like dress reform, its proponents sought to liberate the American woman. "We freed ourselves from the chains of the choking collar and the trailing skirt and the restricted waist and the padded hip," declared one impassioned advocate. "Before we start out to reform the world, let us look after our own necessities and uplift the shoe situation, not by high heels but by high motives." Spearheaded by the YWCA's Department of Social Hygiene in 1919, the campaign urged

Women in low-heeled shoes were believed to have better posture than those who wore high heels.

manufacturers to make a shoe "as good to look at as it is comfortable." American women, said the volunteer organization, want to be "healthful" as well as beautiful and would eagerly welcome a shoe whose design incorporated both elements. Surely we, the 400,000 members of the YWCA, can "get together and put over the idea of a proper shoe in the interest of the health and beauty of American women."

Shoe manufacturers responded forthwith. Mindful of their new responsibilities (and 400,000 potential customers), they, too, rallied around the flag of shoe reform, marrying science with fashion to produce a good-looking, correctly fitting shoe. "Style and comfort are not mortal enemies," proudly related the J. & T. Cousins Company, makers of the Modease shoe. "It's a shoe which the smart woman can wear with her most elaborate costumes without feeling any incongruity." Wm. Henne & Company, manufacturers of the Physical Culture shoe, sounded a similar refrain. With the availability of "anatomically perfect, corrective footwear, made the modern way," declared the company in 1920, "it is not necessary to wear unsightly shoes to enjoy real comfort." The makers of Foot Savers went a step further. "Foot Savers are Scientifically Correct but Not Corrective, Accessible and Fashionable," its advertisements proclaimed. "Like a worthy friend, a shoe should fill every requirement—meet every test—it should be worthy of your constant companionship."

Flush with success, the YWCA next trained its sights on the entire well-being of its constituency, urging every woman to assume personal responsibility for the state of her health from the top of her head to the tip of her toes. In light of the war experience, it was time to question "women's philosophy of life," declared Dr. Bertine. "The pasty-faced, candy-eating girl, who is willing to jog along through life with pains and aches of all kinds has got to change her attitude toward physical health." The best place to start was with the feet. "Good feet, good posture, good shoes, straight-front walking and exercise . . . are *the* foundation for good health," explained the Y's *Handbook on Positive Health* in 1922, counseling readers to pay particular attention to their toes. Did their toes have "power or life"? Were they "crowded against, over, or under each other? Could they pick up pencils?" To ensure the health and well-being of the toe muscles, the United States Public Health Service, for its part, suggested the following exercise: "Work the toes up and down over the edge of a thick board thirty (30) times daily. Stand with feet parallel and somewhat apart with great toes firmly gripping the ground. Without bending the knees or moving the foot, rotate the thighs outward repeatedly. This is chiefly done by strong contraction of the great muscles of the back of the thigh and seat."

American men watched carefully as the women in their lives embraced exercise and the well-fitting shoe, and before long they made shoe reform their cause as well by declaring all-out "war against tight shoes." Male consumers, too, needed to be alerted to the dangers of poor-fitting shoes, explained one of the campaign's architects, Dr. Solomon Strouse of Chicago, noting how most men, having reverted back to their peacetime selves, tended to buy a pair of shoes as if they were buying a tie. Once made aware of the evils of the tight shoe, though, the American male was sure to revolt and to demand change. After all, concluded the good doctor, if tight corsets had succumbed to adverse public opinion, there was every reason to believe that tight shoes would suffer a similar fate, "emancipating two sexes this time, instead of only one."

Strouse's optimism turned out to be premature. True, the public had awakened to the importance of properly fitting shoes; this concern, as one shoe salesman reported in 1920, was very much in the air. Within a few years, though, it faded away. While men were doing far better than they had before, women still refused to give up their high heels, lamented Dr. Dudley J. Morton, author of a popular 1939 advice book, *Oh, Doctor! My Feet!*, a volume

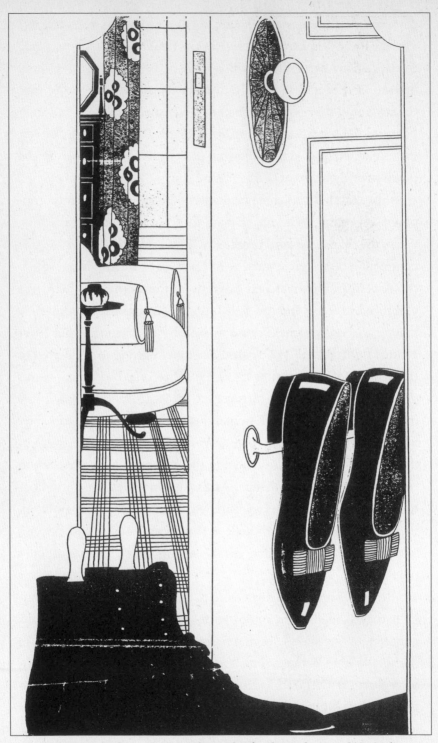

Adorning the foot or hugging the inside of a closet, shoes could be both
beautiful and practical.

intended to "start people thinking—thinking and talking—about an extraordinary situation—their feet." Most people knew very little about their lower extremities and what they did know came from advertisements, he observed, determined to reverse this sorry state of affairs. Along the way, he had much to say about the struggle between looks and comfort, especially when high heels were at issue. Positing something akin to a categorical imperative, Morton believed that all women had an affinity for high heels. Short women liked high heels because they increased their height, he explained; tall women liked high heels because they made their feet look smaller. "And all women want them because they seem to accentuate the arch and beautify the foot." Doctors, scientists, and shoe salesmen might fume and fret but there was very little to be done about the situation, Morton gamely acknowledged: "High heels cannot be legislated out of existence any more than bobbed hair, cosmetics or liquor can be." Their pull was just too strong. At best, the "normally vain" woman was prepared to compromise, reserving high heels for dress and sensible shoes for everyday wear or, as a writer for the *New York Times* Sunday magazine mordantly put it, for those occasions when she was either out for a five-mile walk or "dead sure no one was looking."

Forced to choose between being stylish or being sensible, the American woman eventually cast her vote in favor of fashion. From her perspective, shoes had little to do with practicality. Each new pair, she believed, was an "event," intimately bound up with an inner sense of comfort and self-satisfaction and the "mild and harmless conceits" of the self.

The August Sale
of
furs

Authentic
New Modes
for the Season
of
1920-1921

Chandler & Co.
Boston

Once a luxury, furs became increasingly affordable in America of the 1920s.

~

CHAPTER SIX

The Truth about Fur

"Fur-fur-fur: never was the temptation greater to sink your chin into its soft luxuriousness or wrap yourself in its opulent folds than today," trilled one fashion editor in December 1919. And she was right. Fur-fur-fur had taken the American population by storm, transforming entire stretches of Main Street into what looked like a "procession of wild beasts." An increasingly affordable commodity, fur became a popular topic of conversation as well. Wondering whether wearing a fur coat was to be celebrated or decried, hailed as a symbol of economic success or pilloried as a sign of moral decay, Americans plumbed the meaning of mink. No longer the exclusive preserve of the wealthy or an heirloom passed down from one generation to the next, a fur coat was now available to the many. Mink, sable, and silver fox still remained

STYLE U.

Gents' Overcoat lined and trimmed with Mink, Beaver or Otter, $100, $125, $150, $175, $200.

Muskrat lined, $50.00, $65.00, $75.00.

Sealskin Overcoats, $250, $300, $350, $400.

Fur appealed to men as well as women.

outside the realm of possibility for everyone but the moneyed elite (a mink coat, it was said, "does fifty-five hundred dollars worth of damage to a bank account"). But coats fashioned out of muskrat, mole, rabbit, and squirrel skins and ranging in price from under $100 to a high of $250 were well within reach of the aspiring middle class. The wearing of fur, the *New York Times* reported in 1924, had "become universal in all classes of society." Even the working girl made sure to have "at least a touch of fur" on her garments.

Men, too, fell prey to fur's silky appeal. Though fur-lined or fur-trimmed cloth coats had long been an attribute of affluent American men, their college-age sons had taken to wearing fur— and lots of it—on the outside. Before long, the oversize raccoon coat had become the emblem of the dashing, feckless American undergraduate, the "noisy, hey-hey college boy," prompting *Collier's* magazine to observe that, "translated into a coat," the lowly raccoon had done more than his fair share toward "making our great universities what they are today."

Crossing gender and class lines, fur even transcended the weather, as "summer furs" became fashionable. Avid fur fanciers no longer had cause to regret the arrival of spring and summer; they could now supplement their winter fur wardrobes with loose and lightweight evening wraps or "coatees," abbreviated fur coats or jackets that "came in like a cyclone" and swept the American public off its feet. Some, of course, conceded the incongruity of a fur coat worn in July. "If our grandmothers could only see us wearing furs in summer, they would believe their offspring had lost their mind," acknowledged Florence Rose, a fan of the summer fur. Even so, changeable weather ("It doesn't always stay hot for long") plus personal comfort ("A summer fur takes away the chill of a summer evening") made them a sensible form of attire, she reported.

Innovations in the dyeing and dressing of skins fueled

A mink coat was as sleek and stylish as the flapper who wore one.

America's demand for summer furs and other novelties. New techniques in dyeing enabled furriers to make use of furs previously shunned as worthless and unwearable, thus expanding their repertoire of saleable items and "conferring beauty upon a larger mass of people." What's more, furs now came in a broad range of colors, from gunmetal and oyster gray to maple and amber, heightening their appeal to consumers once restricted to a palette of somber browns and blacks. Novel methods of dressing skins, in turn, transformed baggy and ungainly coats into smart and shapely ones that rivaled silk and velvet in suppleness and ease. "Certainly the pliancy of line [and] the great elegance" of contemporary furs were the "supreme achievement in the entire tradition and history of dress," rhapsodized Henri Bendel, owner of the ever so chic Manhattan dress shop that bore his name. "Sumptuous grace rather than expensive bulkiness is a speaking tribute to every craftsman engaged in a [fur's] creation."

Together with Bendel, who insisted that a fur coat was an "indispensable accessory of modern life," fashion's arbiters gleefully embraced the growing popularity of fur. Introducing the "style element" into what had been a relatively tame, even stodgy arena, they made it clear that wearing one's grandmother's fur coat was no longer acceptable. "Out-of-date furs are no more to be tolerated than out-of-date bonnets," they charged, insisting that stylishness was now as "important in peltries as it is in silk, wool," and millinery. Industry spokesmen joined in. There was a "fur for every face [and] figure," they declared, reassuring those who worried about purchasing one of the newer and cheaper furs. For those women anxious lest they look like a "brownie" when clad in a fur, the industry made sure to supply helpful hints on how to select one appropriate to their height and weight. If they were "short, stout and little," such women were told, they should beware of fox. On them, it was "utterly hopeless." Tall and lovely women, on the other hand, had little to fear. Everything looked good on them.

Nutria trimmed with leopard made quite a fashion statement.

Some furriers sought not just to entice but to familiarize consumers with the world of fur. Publishing charts that distinguished among "durable, less durable, and delicate" furs and issuing dictionaries that carefully explained the differences between muskrat and marten, broadtail and Persian lamb, they attempted to transform the American public into the "fur-wise." Retailers, who had much to gain from an educated consumer, released their own compendia of advice. In 1926, for instance, Selbert Ltd., a well-established retailer ("They think furs, talk furs, dream furs") produced *The Fur Book of Knowledge,* a "little book of fur facts" intended for first-time buyers. Full of practical information on what to look for when purchasing a fur and how to care for it (be sure to visit the "fur doctor" at the first sign of moths, the company advised), the volume was designed to take the worry out of owning a fur coat. Not to be outdone, Abraham Gottlieb, a retailer in business for nearly forty years, made sure to publish his own account, which he entitled *Fur Truths: The Story of Furs and the Fur Business.* Apparently, the sage counsel of the Selberts and the Gottliebs won them many converts. By the time their two books appeared, not only did the fur business in the United States account for $100 million in trade but fur coats and cuffs, it seems, had become "about as common as sand in a desert."

Once the fur craze showed few signs of abating, Americans on the street and around the dinner table took to discussing its causes. "In these days, when furs present so interesting a topic of conversation someone is sure to bring [it] up," reported the *Literary Digest* in 1920. Some attributed fur's popularity to the booming economy of the Roaring Twenties. More and more Americans had more and more money in their pockets and were eager to spend it on themselves, they said. Witness the fur coat's appeal to both men and women. No, it was the automobile, said others. As more Americans spent their free time driving around in the great outdoors, they needed something to keep them really warm and only a fur coat would do. Why, it was the radiator, said still others, pointing to another technological marvel of the era. As more Americans grew accustomed to a greater measure of comfort inside their homes, they'd come to expect the same level of coziness when outside. A fur coat was simply the outdoor equivalent of steam heat.

"If you're in love, you'll say it with sables," rhapsodized furrier I. J. Fox.

Fur may have been good for the body and the economy but was it good for the soul? Weren't the moral costs too high? Distinguishing between the legitimate perquisites of comfort and frivolous ornamentation, between protection and "coquettish adornment," a small but growing number of Americans began to question the good judgment of their fur-clad fellow citizens. It was one thing, they grudgingly conceded, to wear a fur coat when temperatures hovered around the freezing mark, but a summer fur? Worn in the heat of August? Clearly, that had little to do with protection against the weather and everything to do with the determination to be "à la mode, no matter the discomfort or the incongruity." Some extended this argument to cover winter furs as well. "It is not for warmth that the majority of furs are worn but in obedience to the instinct of personal adornment," related Minnie Maddern Fiske in the pages of the *Ladies' Home Journal*, urging its readers to renounce both their summer and their winter furs. They were not worn for protection, for "human comfort and health." They were worn simply to satisfy their wearers' vanity. And that was only the half of it. "Millions of refined, sensitive, cultured, generous-hearted women are accomplices after the fact in the ferocious cruelty of trapping," she continued. American women, charged animal-rights activist Lucy Furman in 1928, gave no thought to how their fur coats were obtained. And if, for a second or two, troublesome questions did arise, women thrust them "back into the hinterland of [their] consciousness" and gave them no more thought. Yet the truth was hideous.

Freighted with responsibility for America's fur-buying frenzy, women were also held accountable for the perilous existence of the nation's wildlife. Women's demand for fur was leading straight to animal extinction, claimed Henry Fairfield Osborn, president of the American Museum of Natural History, noting that "nothing in the history of creation has paralleled the ravages of the fur and hide trade." It was only a matter of time before game animals would "be seen only in museums and picture books." But all was not lost. A concerted campaign against fur trapping might save the animal kingdom, the influential museum president suggested. The "close of the Age of Mammals can be arrested through the creation of sound sentiment and the education of women and children."

Little by little, sound sentiment against the conventions of fur wearing began to take hold. In Springfield, Massachusetts, for instance, the American branch of the international humane society, the Blue Cross, launched a campaign against the use of the purely decorative fur in 1925. The society recognized the fur industry as just as legitimate a business as the stockyards, said its president, Maude Phillips. Moreover, it did not want to harm an industry that supported over half a million people. But, seeking the middle ground, it wished to put an end to the "elaborate neckpieces, dangling heads and tails" fancied by hundreds of thousands, to the "excessive use of fur as embellishment." Elsewhere, the American Society for the Prevention of Cruelty to Animals trained its sights on schoolchildren. Through its "Curriculum of Humane Education," it sought to alert young minds to the cruelty of trapping, hoping they would influence their parents to advocate fur farming, which was widely believed to be a far more humane institution than trapping. The most determined and resolute of animal advocates (the "fur antis," as they were called by their opponents) pinned their hopes on a campaign similar to the one mounted by the Audubon Society some thirty years earlier. Then, too, personal embellishment had been at issue, but the moral battle had not been over fur. It had been over feathers.

At a time when airy tufts of aigrette feathers provided the finishing touch to every woman's hat, Harriet Lawrence Hemenway, a Boston grand dame, turned against them. Inviting her friends to tea one day in 1896, she urged them to renounce the plume. Too many herons lost their lives so that women might adorn themselves, she said, appealing to her peers to join her in championing the cause of bird protection. A year later, the Audubon Society was born. No fad or isolated venture, Hemenway and her sister Audubonites explained to anyone willing to listen, protecting the rights of birds was part and parcel of the "movements of the age that make for righteousness."

To drum up support, the Audubon Society appealed to the clergy, encouraging its members to preach on the folly of wearing feathers; those in the pews, meanwhile, were urged to compile "white lists" of milliners prepared to ornament their hats with flowers in lieu of feathers. With dozens of branches across the country, from Massachusetts to Wisconsin, the society was able to throw its collective weight and purchasing power behind these milliners with a conscience and to sponsor exhibitions where featherless bonnets—or "Audubonnets," as they were called—were displayed. Up and down the East Coast, hat shows filled with samples of birdless millinery repeatedly drew audiences of several hundred women who, throughout the winters of 1899 and 1900, braved the weather to show their support. The success of this venture, crowed *Bird-Lore*, the house organ of the Audubon movement, "proved conclusively that the plumage of wild birds can be easily discarded without violating the laws of fashion." When not holding hat shows or meetings designed to get the American woman to "readjust her conscience and her headgear," the Audubon Society adopted sterner measures. It lobbied local lawmakers for legislation to prohibit the importation, processing, and sale of aigrette feathers. Eventually, it cast an even broader net, seeking protection for all birds, with the exception of barnyard

In early-twentieth-century America, feathers provided
the crowning touch to women's hats.

fowl and ostriches, creatures whose lives were not endangered by the harvesting of their feathers. ("Taking plumes from the ostrich," explained *Bird-Lore*, "is no more painful to the bird than shearing is to a sheep.")

For all the support the Audubonites enjoyed from the clergy and the legislature, women were central to the movement, its loyal foot soldiers and moral conscience. Drafting petitions, buttonholing politicians, and cajoling milliners, the society developed an array of programs that appealed strongly to a female constituency and a feminine sensibility. Perhaps its finest hour came in 1906, when the General Federation of Women's Clubs, some 250,000 strong, agreed to consider a resolution in support of their sister organization: "I pledge myself not to wear any such Badge of Cruelty as is the aigrette, or the plumage of any wild bird," affirmed every member, promising as well "to use every possible influence to restrain others from doing so." Women's devotion to the cause, however, went far beyond their pledging allegiance to it. Holding one another morally accountable for "making cemeteries of their heads," they insisted that the wanton slaughter of birds was all their fault. If women had not succumbed to the allure and charm of the majestic feather, if they hadn't been such slavish devotees of fashion, no bird would have lost its life. Off on the sidelines, quite a few men agreed with this assessment. Women were entirely responsible for the slaughter of innocent birds, wrote one aggrieved man in 1910. "And these are the creatures who want to vote?!"

To be sure, some Americans objected vigorously to the idea of women's exclusive culpability. Men were equally guilty, insisted Alice Stone Blackwell of Dorchester, Massachusetts. The "destruction of birds," she wrote, "is due jointly to men's love of profits and women's love of prettiness." The editor of the *Ladies' Home Journal* agreed, seeking a more equitable distribution of blame and a fairer assessment of responsibility in the first place:

"To accuse women of taking a conscious part in such slaughter . . . is carrying the matter beyond the point of reason. A woman knows, of course, that the bird which decorates her hat must, at some time, have had the breath of life in it. But that the feathered songster was solely, and with premeditation, killed so that her hat might be more decorative or fashionable, does not, I think, occur to her. She simply does not think of it at all. She purchases a hat with a bird perched upon it with as little thought as she buys the material for her woolen gloves."

But this was precisely the point that the Audubonites in their Audubonnets sought to put across: women *ought* to have given thought to what they wore. After all, where men thoughtlessly blundered their way through life, women generally did not, or so common wisdom had it. Believed to be far more sensible and "tender-hearted," far more considerate and thoughtful, far more morally attuned than their husbands, brothers, and sons, women had no excuse for not thinking about what they put on their heads. Most to be faulted were women of refinement, what one writer in *Bird-Lore* called "really nice people." Surely no lady would be found sporting feathers on her hat, a Mrs. G. B. Satterlee wrote to the *Times*, making it categorically clear that eschewing feathers had as much to do with social class as with female character. By her lights and those of the women of the Audubon Society, the truly refined were certain to swear off feathers as a matter of course (and principle) while women further down the social scale, those whom the society mockingly referred to as the "real loidies," who wore "rings instead of gloves, haunted the cheaper shops . . . chewed gum and expectorated with seeming relish," would not. Distinguishing between the real loidy and the true lady, the society's members seemed intent on making social class as much the issue as the well-being of the nation's birds.

At first, whatever animus the movement might have held toward the feather-brandishing hoi polloi remained beneath the surface. But as matters wore on, the Audubon Society increasingly took potshots at the ethnicity as well as the social class of its opponents. "The foreign-born part of our cosmopolitan population are giving the Association a great deal of trouble and some hard work," related *Bird-Lore* in a 1905 article entitled, simply, "Aliens." "They seem to have an inconquerable desire to kill something, and no respect for the laws." "They," of course, referred to the "commercial interests," the "Broadway feather-dealers"—the Jews who made up a disproportionately large number of those employed in the feather industry. Against such people, insisted the members of the Audubon Society, appeals in Mother Nature's behalf simply fell flat; their commercial instincts were too strong. The society also took to couching its campaign in the unassailable terms of patriotism, baldly hinting that those who opposed them were un-American as well as impervious to nature's charms. Essentially, it all came down to the same thing. Conflating patriotism with the cause of bird protection, the Audubon Society insisted that it was the duty of every woman and man in the land to "join in the great civic movement to preserve the wild life of the country. Surely love of country," the society said, "embraces within its meaning a love for its natural beauty."

Their patriotism, integrity, and better natures impugned, feather retailers and importers, together with their allies in the millinery business, went on the attack. "We must take up the gauntlet and meet these people in a battle royal," they thundered. Claiming to love America as much as, if not more than, the members of the Audubon Society—after all, didn't companies such as J. H. Rosenstein and B. Schapiro provide jobs for over fifteen thousand of their fellow Americans—the feather interests worked behind the scenes to challenge the legality of the Audubon Society's efforts. Dismissing the society as a bunch of "self-righteous," "over-zealous," and "misguided sentimentalists," they turned to the courts, where, entangled in a thicket of interpretation, their lawyers tested the limits of the law: Were all feathers to be outlawed or just those belonging to local birds? And what of those winged creatures who migrated annually from the Old World to the New? Were they, too, under the protection of the United States authorities? (This query prompted one bird protector to wonder: "Who furnishes birds with passports and protective papers of citizenship that the plume hunters shall respect?")

The feather trade and its supporters also made effective use of the court of public opinion, framing their approach in terms of personal liberty. And what could be more high-minded, more American than that? The Audubonites were so busy protecting the rights of birds, charged the "commercial interests," they lost sight of the rights of those of us here on earth, especially women's right to choose to wear a feather. Feathers were lovely to behold; unlike fruits, berries, and ribbons, which also ornamented women's hats, they "continually [took] new form and had the charm of motion as well as of rich beauty." Was it just to deny women their right to such pleasure or their right to determine what they should wear?

The debate between those who placed the rights of animals above their own and those who did not lasted for years. Ultimately, the Audubonites carried the day. Having succeeded in calling the nation's attention to the plight of its avian wildlife, they also succeeded, by 1910, in making aigrettes illegal. Feather wearing, however, remained in vogue for a few more years, at least until the doyennes of fashion in postwar America put away their feathers and put on a sleek, streamlined cloche. In the meantime, faux aigrettes like the Neargrette and the so-called Audubon aigrette, an "imitation aigrette which violates no laws and can be sold in every state" (it was fashioned from the feathers of barnyard animals), enjoyed considerable popularity. So, too, did the

COPYRIGHT 1909

THE LEADERS IN THE LINE

Ostrich Plumes :-: Willows
Willow Bands :-: Novelties
:-: Shower-Pompons :-:

Short Heavy-head Plumes Our Specialty.

PH. ADELSON & BRO.
625 BROADWAY NEW YORK

PARIS   ESTABLISHED 1873   LONDON

Ostrich feathers eventually replaced aigrettes as the plumes of choice.

prohibitively expensive ostrich feather, now the plume of choice, and the tufts of its less respectable but more affordable cousins the turkey, the pheasant, and the chicken. But then, the Audubon Society's greatest legacy was strategic rather than sartorial. Forging an alliance between the "law and the lady," the Audubon Society taught Americans how to go about the business of moral education.

Postwar "crusaders against cruelty," not surprisingly, looked to the Audubon Society and its antifeathers campaign as a guiding light. Keen students of the past, they borrowed elements of the society's rhetoric, many of its tactics and all of its moral certitude to alert the nation to the underside of the fur craze. To whip up enthusiasm for the cause, activist Lucy Furman, for example, took to the pages of *The Atlantic Monthly* in February 1928 to describe how her own "aigrette-crazy" generation had eventually come to its senses. Once the American woman learned how these feathers were so cruelly obtained, she vowed to eschew them and "after a few years an aigrette was never seen," Furman related, hopeful that the contemporary American woman would also awaken to the evils of fur trapping. "Fashion is not altogether our god," she pointed out. "We are capable of dropping a style like a hot cake when we know that at its root is something iniquitous." Why not join with her, then, in supporting the work of the Anti-Steel-Trap League, she concluded, appealing directly to the magazine's female readers. "I believe that no class of woman will be so ready and so able to take hold of this evil of steel-trapping and put an end to the most outstanding atrocity of modern times as the thinking women who read the Atlantic."

The Anti-Steel-Trap League, a membership organization based in Washington, D.C., had formed in 1925 to arouse the nation's conscience to the ills of an instrument whose cruelty reportedly surpassed "even the horrors of the Inquisition." The steel trap was an affront to all right-thinking Christians and "should not be tolerated in a Christian civilization," the league's supporters insisted, infusing their cause with the holy zeal of religion. Calling cruelty to animals an "act of essential sinfulness," the league inquired: "What Are *You* Doing to Help?" Were people writing letters to newspapers expressing their opposition to steel traps? Were they urging friends and neighbors to wear farmed furs? Were they recruiting members to the Anti-Steel-Trap League?

Through the presentation of a new kind of nature story in

MEMBERSHIP APPLICATION

I desire to join the Anti-Steel-Trap League, Incorporated, Washington, D. C., a National Organization to Outlaw Steel-Traps, and enclose herewith $................

NAME..
(State whether Mr., Mrs. or Miss)

No. and Street..

City..State....................

ALL DONORS BECOME MEMBERS
Make checks payable to Anti-Steel-Trap League, Incorporated
1731 K St. N.W., Washington, D. C.
No Paid Officers

PLEDGE

Never buy any fur which has the faintest suspicion of the Steel-Trap about it. You need be in no fear, in doing this, of hurting either the trapper or the fur dealer; you will lighten your conscience; you will encourage the humane production of fur-bearing animals; and you will help to rid your country of the heinous crime of allowing millions upon millions of warm-blooded animals to be foully tortured to death every year in the atrocious Steel-Trap.

I PLEDGE MYSELF TO DO THIS HUMANE THING

(Signed) ....

No. and Street....................................City......................State................

ALL DONORS BECOME MEMBERS
Anti-Steel-Trap League, Incorporated, 1731 K Street N.W., Washington, D. C.

Members of the Anti-Steel-Trap League called on their fellow citizens
to support their cause.

which America's fabled backwoods were the modern mise-en-scene of untold cruelty, the league hoped to win the public's assent for a more humane form of trapping, one in which the animals suffered little or hardly at all. Its crusade was not just for women, the league's officers reassured potential male members. Nor was it for the faint of heart. Many people seemed to think that "men engaged in humane work, and in what the loose thinking generally call 'uplifting,' are as a rule of an effeminate, if not a weakling nature." But that was emphatically not the case, the league insisted, boasting of the many men of valor on its rolls: scientists, biologists, physicians, and war heroes like the league's founder, Edward Breck. Boy Scouts, too, had rallied to the cause, acting on the Sixth Scout Rule: "A Scout is kind to animals."

Even so, women bore the lion's share of responsibility for the league's work. Rallying the troops, they raised money and secured the support of new friends like the Margaret Brent Civic Guild, a Massachusetts organization of lay Catholic women, and old ones like the General Federation of Women's Clubs, which once again lent its imprimatur to the cause of animal rights. Some women, their hearts inflamed by the injustice of it all, even took to writing poems like this one, which appeared in the *Anti-Steel-Trap League News* of May 1931:

> *Who killed Brer Rabbit?*
> *"Why I!" said Dame Fashion.*
> *"Since furs are my passion,*
> *I killed Brer Rabbit."*

> *Who helped and abetted?*
> *"We, we!" cried her daughters*
> *"We called for the slaughters!*
> *We helped and abetted."*

Still, for all its fervor, the Anti-Steel-Trap League never enjoyed the good fortune or, for that matter, the stature of the Audubon Society. In truth, it never had much of a chance. Pitted against the great American pastime of hunting, that manly sport, the league met with only limited success on the legislative front. A number of states—Georgia, South Carolina, and Kentucky among them—passed legislation outlawing steel traps. Most, however, did not. Nor did the league manage to tug at the nation's heartstrings as effectively as the Audubon Society had once done. Time and again, its efforts fell short. In mounting frustration by the mid-1930s, the organization had shifted gears. Having claimed all along not to be antifur so much as anti–steel trap, it abandoned that position. No longer did the league condone the wearing of fur provided it was killed in a humane way. Instead, it urged its supporters to refrain from wearing fur altogether: "Don't ask for any furs for Christmas—and don't give any," it counseled. "Christmas will have more good will without a gift that caused a living creature to scream in pain."

But even that change of heart (and strategy) was too late to prevent the Anti-Steel-Trap League from losing ground. Fur farming was well on its way to becoming a viable alternative to trapping, rendering calls for a more humane form of trapping all but moot while assuaging the consciences of those concerned about animal cruelty. In 1917, for instance, there were only four fur farms in the entire United States; by 1930, there were more than forty-five hundred. When wild animals like mink, muskrat, and fox were no longer hunted down but "coddled almost as much as a millionaire's son," what need was there for an anti-steel-trap league? More pointedly still, the outbreak of World War II pushed anticruelty campaigns like this one to the margins of the nation's consciousness. It was hard to talk about cruelty to animals when confronting daily examples of man's inhumanity to man. As for those opposed to wearing fur of any kind, wild or farmed, theirs was truly an uphill battle. Well into the war years, fur continued to exert its magic pull. America's "peltry" was "thriving," gleefully declared *Business Week* in 1941, pointing to declining prices and skyrocketing sales. Furs continued to "go democratic." Another commentator of the time, one Elizabeth Frazer, musing on the social significance rather than the economics of fur's continued popularity, wondered whether there wasn't something in the American character that might explain fur's profound hold. After all, fur trapping and fur wearing had a long history in this country, dating to the early years of the republic, and then some. "Furs give us pleasure!" she pronounced. "Love of them lies deep in the very blood of the race."

Frazer was on to something. But it had nothing to do with blood or race and everything to do with America. Transcending the circumstances of its birth, a fur coat symbolized America's bounty and beauty. A fur coat bore witness to the promise of America. In homes across the nation, especially those inhabited by immigrants and their children, the purchase of a fur coat was experienced not as a failure of will or as a sign of moral turpitude. It was experienced as a triumph and a vindication, as material evidence of America's blessings. "A fur coat is the achievement of a decade of yearning," explained Ruth Glazer, writing of her immigrant parents and their friends who delighted in their hard-won mink-dyed muskrats. "It would be a shame if people didn't notice."

The giving of jewelry at Christmas became an American tradition.

CHAPTER SEVEN

Say It with Jewelry

Women have a special affinity for jewelry, declared *Vogue* in 1910. Eight out of ten of them found "the jeweler's window surpasses in interest the most artfully decorated show case in the dry goods shop, or the tempting display of the costumer or milliner." Journalist Muriel MacFarlane was one of those women. "I have not yet steeled myself to withstand the lure of the jewelry store," she confessed. Both MacFarlane and the fashion magazine gave voice to commonly held notions of an indissoluble link between gems and gender. Women and jewelry, it seemed, were meant for each other. But was this a good thing? Did not women's appetite for jewelry run counter to one of America's most cherished articles of faith, its belief in the simple life? And was not too great an interest in jewelry a sign of bad taste, perhaps even of moral laxity? After all, it was widely agreed that "one of the few ways in which a man or a woman unerringly expresses individuality is in the use or misuse of jewelry." Pitting chromosomes against culture and extravagance against restraint, jewelry tested America's belief in the perfectability of human nature and the democracy of good taste.

Back on Main Street, meanwhile, jewelry shops flourished, suggesting that many ordinary Americans rejected the notion that a piece of jewelry might besmirch their character, especially when it came in the form of a gift. By the early years of the twentieth century, the jewelry store had become a neighborhood institution and its proprietor an arbiter of taste whose judgment was to be relied on when one purchased a present. "This *is* a gift-giving age," confirmed etiquette writer Hallie E. Rives, listing the number of occasions—including Easter, Mother's Day, Father's Day, Thanksgiving, christenings, confirmations, graduations, weddings, and "anniversaries of all kinds"—when the exchange of presents was customary. There was "no doubt that the giving of presents gives greater happiness to the human race than almost everything else," added Colonel John Shepard, a champion of gift giving, "for it is by such presents that man gives expression to his love of family, of friends, of art."

Despite Shepard's imprimatur, the practice, indeed the "philosophy," of presents, gave rise to considerable confusion. Then as now, the giving of gifts was fraught with tension, entangling both giver and recipient in a fragile web of intimacy. What constituted an appropriate gift? How much money should one spend? What, wondered *Vogue*, could "one smart woman" possibly give another? America's jewelers leapt into the breach, trumpeting jewelry—pearls for her, onyx studs for him—as the very best kind of gift, the "gift that lasts." "Why not say it with jewelry," they insisted, pointing out that thousands of dollars were squandered each year on "foolish, useless giving," on floral bouquets and overly expensive furs. Flowers wilted and furs molted, but jewelry

Etiquette determined just how much jewelry was too much.

endured. It did not "die with the passing of a day or a season," but lasted, "like the fidelity of a fine friendship, for as long as life itself!" Long-lasting American-made jewelry was also increasingly affordable. With the growth of Newark's jewelry industry in the years following the Civil War—the New Jersey city was the

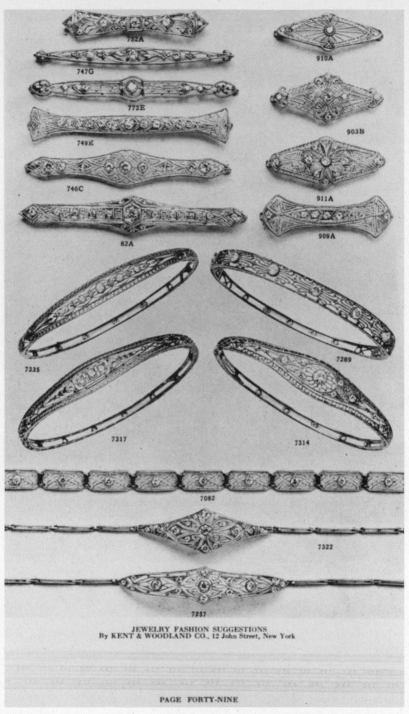

752A

910A

747G

772E

903B

749E

746C

911A

82A

909A

7335

7289

7317

7314

7082

7322

7257

JEWELRY FASHION SUGGESTIONS
By KENT & WOODLAND CO., 12 John Street, New York

The growing availability of affordable jewelry tested the nation's resolve.

"fine jewelry capital of the United States"—more and more Americans found a piece of jewelry within their reach. "The fact that the purse is limited in its buying capacity is not going to deprive the possessor of the joys of wearing jewelry," declared the Bureau of Jewelry Fashions in 1917. "A limitless array of jewelry" was now available for those of moderate means.

American-made jewelry lent itself to a number of different gift-giving opportunities. Christmas topped the list. As the *National Jeweler* explained, "Santa Claus knows that a dollar goes farther at the jewelry store than it does anywhere else in procuring usefulness and pleasure. Ask Santa Claus. He knows!" Assisted by the all-knowing jeweler (and Santa), shoppers eagerly filled their stockings with "interesting insect jewelry" and strings of pearls. ("Nothing can take the place of pearls.") Men's Christmas needs could also be met by a visit to the local jewelry store. "As a boon to the woman who shops and the man who receives, the masculine members of society have not been neglected," noted one industry spokesman. Gold or silver belt buckles of "substantial quality and mannish design" and "sturdy, true, dependable" wristwatches, all the rage in the years following World War I, made husbands, fathers, and sons feel as suitably bejeweled as the women in their families. Easter, too, began to be seen as a time for giving "dainty articles of personal jewelry." "A gift at Easter is becoming a Custom, as it should," happily noted the *National Jeweler* in 1925, pointing with pride to its stock of jeweled miniature calla lilies and rosary beads that came in as many as nine different styles and twelve different colors. "Thousands are being sold to Catholics."

Marking the holidays, gifts of jewelry also became thoroughly intertwined with personal moments like birthdays and engagements. "Whether she is three or three-score, pearls are a fitting gift," instructed one manufacturer. "People think of pearls when they think of birthdays." Big birthdays like a woman's eighteenth or twenty-first, which celebrated the transition between "youth and ladyhood," were especially treasured. What better way to announce the birthday girl's coming of age than by her donning a string of pearls and enjoying the "privilege of wearing 'real jewelry'"? And what better way to announce a woman's engagement than the all-important diamond solitaire, a gift said to be "purely spontaneous, called forth by affection only"? Although inextricably bound up with the life cycle, this "outward and visible sign of an engagement" was by no means indispensable, conceded Mrs.

Pearls were de rigueur at the Sosnofskys' Passover seder in 1925.

Burton Kingsland, an expert on "Good Manners and Good Form." Undoubtedly, there were many women who never received an engagement ring, and their "compact is none the less sacred." And yet, by the turn of the century, "even the most impulsive girl" did not "really feel properly engaged" until a diamond adorned the fourth finger of her left hand.

Of all jewelry the engagement ring carries the most beautiful sentiment and grows more precious as the years go by.

The Field Solitaire Ring is made with infinite care, is correct in height, perfect in proportion. These beautiful rings display the diamond to the best advantage.

Still, for everyone who fancied a lustrous string of pearls or a proper-size engagement ring ("Fashion," it was said, "rather prefers a large, semi-precious gemstone to a microscopic diamond"), there were those who unhesitatingly believed that wearing jewelry was a perilous enterprise, likely to trap the wearer in the coils of excess. Americans were told by their very own self-appointed "apostles of civility" to be on their guard lest they succumb to the siren call of extravagance and, in the process, sully not only themselves but America, too. Against a steady drumbeat of "Don'ts," women especially were urged to wear jewelry "sparingly," to "avoid burdening [their] fingers with too many rings," "not to dazzle their neighbors," and never, ever to wear diamonds during the day. "It has always been the rule of the well-bred not to wear too many jewels in public places, because public display is considered bad taste in the first place, and in the second, a temptation to a thief," proclaimed the ever-authoritative Emily Post, distinguishing between the truly well-bred and everyone else. Cherishing the notion that the Puritan practice of austerity and restraint was the authentic American way, the truly well-bred and those who spoke for them worried lest an affinity for showy jewelry might somehow render them less American.

By the end of the nineteenth century, public concern with the cultural consequences of extravagance had reached fever pitch. Throughout the 1890s, editorials, books, and even children's short stories repeatedly denounced ostentation, excess, and "conspicuous consumption," the term popularized by the curmudgeonly sociologist Thorstein Veblen in his forcible and witty indictment of contemporary society, *The Theory of the Leisure Class*. "We find things beautiful, as well as serviceable, somewhat in proportion as they are costly," he wrote in 1899, taking his countrymen to task for their slavish devotion to a "pecuniary standard of reputability" in which money was the measure of all things. And nothing better underscored America's fall from grace than the way its citizens dressed: wastefully, extravagantly, and conspicuously. The "function of dress," the sociologist categorically declared, had become little more than "evidence of [the] ability to pay." Veblen, it's true, had his finger on the pulse of America, but in the age of anxiety that was the fin de siècle, many others, like Edward Bok, the influential editor of the *Ladies' Home Journal*, worried alongside him. "We have gone to extremes. We have overdressed. And we have coddled ourselves with the belief that the perversion of good taste is the 'fashionable thing,'" he chided while columnist Helen Watterson Moody (aka "Aunty") warned that "exaggerated ideas" about dress could only lead to no good.

Listening to Washington Gladden's "Santa Claus in the Pulpit" and other cautionary tales, children learned of the perils of extravagance early on. While dozing through a Christmas Day sermon, Mortimer, the story's central character, dreams of coming face-to-face with Santa, who, armed with a "Grand Stereoscopic Moral Tester," reveals the true meaning of Christmas. A beautiful gold necklace is flashed before Mortimer's eyes and those of his friends. "Isn't it a daisy," they say, whereupon Santa urges them to take a closer look. As the "ethical lens" of the Grand Stereoscopic Moral Tester shines its brilliant spotlight on the necklace, the gold links are suddenly transformed into an iron fetter imprisoning the wrists of downtrodden women workers, the employees of the gentleman who purchased the necklace. "It is out of their lifeblood that he is coining his gold," says Santa. "And to think that such a man should take the money that he makes in this way to buy a Christmas present. Ugh!" Ugh, indeed. Ultimately, though, the story ends on a positive note: Mortimer sees the light and realizes not a moment too soon that good taste and restraint go hand in hand.

Thousands of real-life Mortimers felt the same way. They were also given to believing that good taste was a matter of education, not genes. An acquired characteristic, it could be taught, especially to the young. "Good taste is simplicity. That's it, girls, right in a nutshell," said Mrs. Ralston, one sartorial expert, addressing her remarks to teenagers. "I'm not suggesting you dress yourselves like pipe-stems and leave off all your ribbons and bows. Bless your little hearts, I don't mean anything of the kind," she assured her audience. But excessively fussy and "dressed-up clothes" were to be shunned at all costs. If girls heeded her advice, Ralston promised, good taste was sure to follow. Even fathers, if put to the test, could teach their daughters to distinguish between conspicuousness and simplicity. "He may not know much about the technicalities of dress," observed the *Ladies' Home Journal*, "but if he is willing to express the satisfaction that he feels when [his daughter's] gown is suitable . . . he can do much to develop good taste . . . and to make his girls sensible women."

Educators, charged with "getting beauty into the classroom," also bore considerable responsibility for demonstrating how good taste might be acquired, especially when it came to familiarizing America's minorities with the canons of suitability. "To dress in an extravagant, ill-chosen fashion . . . to make either too much or too little of your clothes, is a serious mistake, and one against which I greatly desire to help you guard yourselves," Mrs. M. F. Armstrong told her African American students at the Hampton

Normal and Agricultural Institute, reassuring them that they, too, could learn how not to "overdress." It was wise to avoid dressing "showily," especially when traveling, and at all times to "err on the side of too little color rather than too much." Don't waste your money on trinkets, she counseled, and guard against "the vulgarity of all imitations, false jewelry in particular being always in bad taste." Armstrong concluded by offering this comforting bit of advice: "You will find that among ladies and gentlemen a very plain reality is better than a very fine sham, and that it is good to be true in dress as well as in other things."

Like the students at the Virginia vocational school, America's Jews were also acutely sensitive to the issue of overdressing. Mindful that they were not the only ones to be publicly associated with excess, they laid themselves open all the same to the charge that Jewish women "love jewels more than any other women and display them with greater eagerness than others." Some American Jews, branding these claims as censure, pure and simple, rejected them out of hand. When it came to jewelry, Jewish women had no monopoly, they retorted. "The love for gems and jewels is innate in the heart of [all] women, be they Jewish, Mohammedan or Christian." Others, like the Countess Annie de Montague, saw things differently. For her, the belief that Jewish women adored jewels was entirely justified, but history provided the reason for their passion. "Hebrew women are often reproached with their inordinate love for precious gems," she wrote in 1897, explaining that "this is a heritage from their forefathers, a natural tendency for the brilliant and beautiful." More to the point, there was nothing unseemly about either the heritage or the tendency. "The dark, Oriental beauty of Hebrew women is enhanced by the wearing of flashing jewelry and their love for special ornaments has been fostered by centuries of customs and environments." Still other American Jews, like Rosa Sonneschein, the dashing publisher of the *American Jewess*, the "first American magazine to appeal particularly to Hebrew women," hedged their bets. It wasn't so much that the Jewess had a greater affinity for jewels than other women. It was that her personality was "rather showy and even a modest spread of jewelry tended to make her look vulgar."

Invoking the claims of history and anthropology, however, went only so far in assuaging the community's anxiety. It probably made matters worse, in fact, by implying that extravagance and showiness were innate and immutable Jewish characteristics. But American Jews, determined to feel at home in the New World, could not accept that; even the faintest smudge of suspicion that they remained outside the pale of Western civilization and under the "spell of Eastern fancies" was intolerable. And so they set out to prove by word, deed, and dress that they were just as American as anyone else. Gustav Gottheil, a leading Reform rabbi, affirmed that the "ruling traits of the genus Jewess," like those of her well-bred Christian sister, included "simplicity of manners, modesty . . . economy, cheerfulness, piety, and charity." The *American Jewess* went Gottheil one better. "Under the banner of the Stars and Stripes, that proud and potent emblem of human liberty," proclaimed the magazine's publisher, "the physical characteristics of the Jews have visibly improved. . . . On the average, American Jewesses are beginning to closely resemble other women in their appearance."

Indeed, they not only looked like other Americans but shared their values as well, insisted Sonneschein. Loyal to the core, American Jewish women loved their country deeply, so deeply they were willing to sacrifice all their gold and jewels "as readily as the ancient Jewess did for her religion," declared the publisher, in her enthusiasm misguidedly applying the biblical story of the golden calf to late-nineteenth-century America. Still, that is precisely what American Jewish women did: they "sacrificed at the

Where vos Moses?

Anti-Jewish sentiment made much of the Jewish woman's alleged affinity for excess.

shrine of frivolity." Instituting a modern form of sumptuary legislation no less potent for being voluntary as well as lay-based, American Jewish women drew on the gentle art of persuasion and a female network of support. Through word of mouth, at synagogue sisterhood meetings and annual conventions, and in the pages of the press, they urged one another to act "more like violets and less like sunflowers." They would "conquer [their] innate desire" for jewelry by "cultivating unobtrusive modesty," "strenuously avoiding all ostentatious displays," and wearing jewelry in moderation. Better still, they would boycott it altogether. What clearer proof could there be of their true-blue American-ness?

The community's efforts at sartorial reform seemed to pay off. Happily, the *American Jewess* reported sightings in St. Louis and Chicago of modestly clad Jewish women at fancy-dress balls. "There is not the slightest doubt . . . that American Jewesses understand the art of dressing to perfection," the monthly proudly informed its readers in 1899. "Beauty was arrayed in taste and refinement. No flashing jewelry marred the harmony of the toute ensemble." Cause for equal amounts of approbation and relief, such sightings also prompted the newspaper to publish an extended editorial on the relationship between Jewish women and jewelry. The piece, fusing sociology with moral fervor, applauded the latter-day Jewish woman for having stood history on its head by embracing the American aesthetic of restraint: "Heaven be praised, that jewels are no longer synonymous with Jewess." At long last, she had come to recognize that "the rich tints of her coloring and the brilliancy of her eyes do not need to be accentuated by glittering tinsels. . . . All hail this new American beauty, who, satisfied with her natural, God-given endowments, discards flashing ornamentation." All hail!

American Jewry's sense of triumph, however, soon gave way to consternation. With the arrival of hundreds of thousands of female Jewish immigrants from Eastern Europe a few years later, Jewish women once again stood accused in the dock of public opinion for their overly exuberant, "shrieking" style of dress. The immigrant Jewish girl—the "ghetto girl," writer Fannie Hurst (and others) called her, as if she were some kind of ideal type—was widely believed to cut an extravagant figure. Given to gaudiness and glitter, the ghetto girl reportedly lacked the "restraining force of instinctive good taste"; without it, she couldn't help herself and was inevitably driven to extremes.

Profiled and lampooned in the Yiddish and Anglo-Jewish press, the overly showy and crude immigrant Jewish woman was also immortalized in novels like Abraham Cahan's *The Rise of David Levinsky* where she appears in the guise of Auntie Yetta, whose "flashing" fingers are likened to a "veritable jewelry store."

Did Auntie Yetta really exist? Did Jewish immigrant women lack refinement? And what of their American-born daughters? Did they, too, suffer from flashing fingers? Eager to confront the issue head-on and, hopefully, to lay to rest the notion that Jewish women were constitutionally unable to cultivate restraint, the *American Weekly Jewish News* (a "live, honest and fearless Jewish newspaper") organized a five-way discussion in 1918, soliciting the opinions of those who it believed were in the position to speak authoritatively about such matters. Invited guests included Mrs. Sholom Asch ("She's the wife of one of our foremost Yiddish writers" and, besides, "is always in a Yiddish 'atmosphere'"); Mme. Nazimova, the actress; Foshko, the cartoonist at *Der Tog,* a popular Yiddish daily; Sophie Irene Loeb, a columnist for the *New York Evening World;* and Fannie Hurst ("a real student of humanity, a Jewess and a famous author"). The East Side girl, the participants agreed, had much to learn about the elegance of restraint. Her dress was "hopelessly vulgar and stupid," her makeup "indiscriminate and tasteless," and her coiffure simply "awful." But was the situation beyond repair? Was ostentation and excess an innate Jewish trait, a strain of behavior resistant to change? Or was it a momentary aberration, a transient consequence of living in new and unfamiliar surroundings?

Four of the five experts quickly arrived at a consensus: bad taste, they maintained, was not an inherent trait of character but an "imposition of circumstance," an artifact of history. It was only a matter of time before Jewish women shook off their propensity for clothing that "glared," insisted Mr. Foshko, prompting Mrs. Asch to add, "This crudity will pass with the generation which created it. Gradually, the East-side woman will learn, and when she will have learned and found herself, there will then be no need to write articles on the vulgarity of some East-side girls." America would triumph, Sophie Irene Loeb agreed. While there was a "certain amount of crude dressing on the East Side," it was by no means an innately Jewish characteristic. Once better educated and exposed to higher things, immigrant women would surely develop "good taste in dressing. What showiness these girls exhibit is but the elementary stage in the acquirement of this education." Besides, Loeb hastened to add, dress was not the only measure of a person's virtue. "Go into any library on the East Side and you will find the young people reading Shakespeare and Ibsen. Does this show bad taste?" Mme. Nazimova was equally optimistic about the future. From her perspective, the Jewish woman's "leaning toward over-dressing" and her "showy exhibition of gems and golden trinkets" were a consequence of oppression, not character. "Forbidden all paths, shut out from all social doors, the natural instinct for attracting notice had to find an outlet. It found it in too great an accentuation on personal adornment." But in the New World, where conditions were far more open, Jewish women would surely avail themselves of the opportunity to be as refined as their non-Jewish counterparts; of this she was fairly certain.

Fannie Hurst, however, would have none of it. Bad taste, she hotly insisted, was no accident of history or of timing. It was due, she said, "to the vivid, aggressive temperament and imagination of the Jew" and was not likely to change. Even the most affluent and well-heeled Jewish women suffered from it: "I find this trait in all circles of Jewish society. When I happen to be at some fashionable and wealthy affair I find that the woman who is most over-dressed—most lacking in refinement—is the Jewish woman." Still, the situation was not entirely hopeless, Hurst reluctantly conceded. What they lacked in taste, the Jews more than made up for in positive traits. "When I go down to the East-side and look upon those pasty, white faces and hopelessly vulgar, stupid dresses, I am filled with wonder and admiration that these girls, with all their vulgarity, should rise to the heights that some of them do and be so great in achievement."

With its conflicting, and seemingly irresolvable, references to circumstance, temperament, instinct, and education, this discussion about the origins of taste doubtless comforted some American Jewish readers and left others feeling disturbed, perhaps even a bit uneasy. Chances are, though, that most, if asked, would have sided with Mrs. Asch rather than with Fannie Hurst: too much was at stake not to root for nurture over nature. Eager to demonstrate that they understood, and abided by, the "laws which govern good taste," American Jews read clothes, like tea leaves, for signs that Americanization had successfully taken hold, inside as well as out. Dressing quietly and with restraint bespoke their assimilability; flashy ornamentation, in contrast, set them apart. No wonder, then, that American Jews put their faith in the laws of good taste and sought to live up to its strictures. From where they stood, at the margins of society, to believe in good taste, after all, was to believe in America and its gifts, especially the gift of perfectability, the triumph of environment over history. Surprisingly enough, none other than Emily Post tended to agree. People were apt to think of taste as an inherited trait, America's supreme arbiter wrote in 1936 in response to a reader's query about its origins: "one has it or one hasn't." But the fact of the matter, she continued encouragingly, was that good taste, like an appreciation for music or art, could be developed. That so many Americans were not born with it or exposed to it in childhood should not stand in the way of their acquiring it at a later stage. "Good taste is pouring over our land," she said, citing evidence in department stores, shop windows, homes, and classrooms. "And all this means— what? Merely one more incident added to a great many facts that prove us a wonderful nation."

❧

Emphatically Modern

Every once in a while, reported *Time* magazine in December 1944, New York's Museum of Modern Art staged a "strange, but provocative show" that set people's tongues wagging. *Are Clothes Modern?* it declared, was that kind of show. With displays of bustles and bloomers, shoes and hats, cave drawings of the female form juxtaposed against sketches from *Harper's Bazaar* ("You can't tell them apart and they both look terrible," related one viewer), and sections on "Trousers versus Skirts," "Excess and Superfluity," and "Footwear without Tears," the exhibition cast a glaring spotlight on Americans and their clothing. It gave "Dame Fashion a black eye," frankly observed the *Kingston Leader*, one of many newspapers throughout the country that reported on the exhibition. Curated by the Viennese-born architect Bernard Rudofsky, a self-styled "expert on the superfluousness of buttons and fake pockets" (buttons, he insisted, were little better than fungi), *Are Clothes Modern?* examined clothing as rigorously as a chemist analyzed the elements or an architect studied a building. A great success, the exhibition subsequently traveled to several other cities, where, reported one museum official, it was "violently popular." Obviously touching a nerve, *Are Clothes Modern?* raised questions about the way Americans dressed, suggesting that what they put on their backs was definitely behind the times, "uneconomical, irrational, unaesthetic, and, not to put too fine a point on it, bad." It also hinted at the far-reaching changes likely to take place in the postwar era, changes that would make the sartorial practices—and values—of the previous half century seem as distant as the cave drawings that graced the museum's galleries.

For one thing, by the time the exhibition opened its doors, Americans had already begun to dress differently, less formally, than their parents. Where their mothers were usually skirted, hatted, and high-heeled and their fathers suited and somberly tied, those who came of age during the Second World War pursued a new course. They had become "emphatically" modern. In what was surely the most dramatic and evident index of change, more and more women had begun to wear pants, going far beyond anything Flapper Jane had ever thought possible. "Girls will be boys," proclaimed the *New York Times* in 1940, a bit baffled by the growing number of fresh-faced young women clad in their father's flannel trousers and tweed jackets. The wartime climate had evidently led many to feel there was "no place for frills" and to favor "sturdy masculine common sense," the paper explained, trying valiantly to account for this recent development. Little by little, the sight of women in pants became more acceptable, less startling, especially once World War II was in full throttle. By then, women clad in loose-fitting, deep-pocketed one-piece suits designed by Vera Maxwell and sleek plastic helmets fashioned by Lilly Daché gamely reported to work at the Alameda Naval Station and the Sperry Gyroscope Company, changing America's sartorial as well as economic landscape in the process. Pants, or "slacks," as merchandisers preferred to call them to distinguish them from men's apparel, also took hold outside the factory gates as growing numbers of women, from those in "Garbo and Hepburn sizes" to those who wore a large-size 42, expressed interest in purchasing a pair or two. To meet the demand, Filene's opened several Slack Bars; Detroit's leading department store, J. L. Hudson, added a Trouser Shop for Women, and Marshall Field's in Chicago reported that sales were "zooming all the time." *Vogue*, too, threw its weight behind women's trousers. Publishing a "Primer on Pants," it sought to allay the concerns of those women skittish about wearing them. In reassuring, measured tones, the magazine discussed where to purchase a pair, when to wear them, and how ("with simple jewelry, low-heeled shoes and unself-consciously"). "Slacks look wonderfully well when they're right, incredibly bad when they're wrong," it cautioned.

A symbol of the postwar era, women's pants reflected a growing fascination with the casual life. Calling it a "generational phenomenon, like the Twenties," one student of the fifties suggested that the appeal of the casual had to do with suburbanization, "unostentation," and growing resistance to "physical restraints." In Chicago, for example, researchers for the *Tribune* discovered that all women, "whether living in the heart of the city or on its outskirts, whether over 50 or under 30, whether the hale sportswoman or the delicate houseplant, are changing their wardrobes toward the casual mode." Nothing if not versatile, casual clothing could be worn "while working lightly and neatly around the house or shopping in the neighborhood or attending a PTA meeting." Men, too, adjusted their sartorial standards. "Get casual, man!" exhorted *Newsweek* in 1953, noting a trend toward a more relaxed form of male attire. Sometimes it took the form of a suit made out of new synthetic fabrics, the much-touted wash-and-wear suit that represented the "marriage of Orlon and Dacron." At other moments it took the form of shorts, Bermuda shorts, the kind that fell "precisely two inches above the center of the kneecap." "Giving a leg up—in this case, more appropriately, a knee-up—to historians yet unborn, we wish to record that as of midsummer, 1954, the wearing of shorts by men in New York City no longer seems merely freakish or perverse," commented the *New Yorker*, making sure posterity would know about it. Others, of course, bemoaned the existence of the "beshorted businessman." Ever since the war, American males have been growing lax about their clothes, lamented Emanuel Weinstein, president of the Formal Wear Institute, an organization founded in 1951 by a band of menswear manufacturers "alarmed over the male tendency" to ignore the conventions of gentlemanliness. "It has got so the man in a tuxedo . . . feels he's out of place."

While the sight of men in shorts made Weinstein and his confreres long for the old days, the zoot suit sounded the death knell for gentlemanliness. Adopted by young African Americans, Mexican Americans, and aspiring hepcats, the outfit spoke of freedom and release rather than restraint and control. (The term itself, with its origins in urban jazz culture, connoted exaggeration.) Despite its unusual proportions and snug fit—the jacket hugged the knees while the trousers were so tightly pegged at the bottom that a shoehorn was required to help poke the feet through—the zoot suit, according to social worker Fritz Redl, was a "declaration of independence." While some observers claimed that the suit's long lines were inspired by the Civil War–era garb worn by Clark Gable in *Gone with the Wind*, the very first one on record was ordered in February 1940 by Clyde Duncan, an African American busboy from Gainesville, Georgia. "I thought it was as crazy as could be," reported A. C. McEver, the tailor who assembled the zoot suit from Duncan's specifications. He tried to talk Duncan out of it, he said, but the young man was stubborn. At first,

McEver and his colleagues in the menswear industry believed the ensemble to be just a passing fancy, a singular idiosyncrasy. They assumed that Duncan was "one of those whimsical people who turn up at a tailor's occasionally with extraordinary ideas" and let it go at that. But the industry was taken by surprise when the zoot suit caught on in New Orleans, Mississippi, and Alabama, then leapfrogged to Harlem before spreading across the country.

The new casual spirit soon settled on the sanctuary as well as the street. By the late fifties and early sixties more and more worshipers began to shun their good clothes in favor of open-necked shirts and other forms of casual dress, prompting a dismayed rabbi to observe that when he looked out upon his congregation one Sabbath morning, "Behold, the bar mitzvah, his family and his friends were attired as if the synagogue were the first link on the golf course." As those in the pews increasingly placed more of a premium on ease and comfort than on the strictures of respectability and stylishness, hats, too, tumbled from grace, especially among women. Wearing one, complained a Catholic priest, had become "the unusual thing." Instead, Catholic women either went without or made do with a handkerchief, a hair bow, or a "wisp of a veil." Jewish women bound for synagogue followed suit, perching a lace doily (purists called it a "chapel cap") atop their heads or donning a yarmulke. Such improvisations did not sit well with America's clergymen. Ill-prepared to countenance, let alone welcome, these displays of makeshift millinery, they not only denounced them (the yarmulke was for men, not women, said one Brooklyn rabbi categorically), they wrote to their superiors seeking advice. Having railed against the presence of big hats, they now found themselves in the odd position of missing them. "Is there any basis for tolerating the modern custom of women not wearing any head covering in church?" asked one priest who styled himself "Semper Confusus." Did this growing custom abrogate canon law? No, it did not, he was firmly told. Though women were expected to provide themselves with proper head covering when they came to church, under "certain circumstances a slight deviation from the usual custom" might be allowed. Clergymen, too, began to loosen their collars, literally as well as metaphorically. "Our children are seeking authenticity and for them, robes are a symbol of the aura of the sanctimonious establishment," wrote Los Angeles rabbi Hillel Silverman, explaining his decision to retire his ceremonial robe. Without it, he felt "very much more at ease—natural and comfortable." Some Catholic priests, meanwhile, experimented with leaving off their clerical dress or retaining only a part of it when they were not officiating at a prayer service.

The most far-reaching change of all, though, was attitudinal rather than material. Clothes no longer mattered. It was not that Americans in the 1950s and 1960s stopped caring about what they wore or how they looked. On the contrary, they cared a great deal, wondering how to appear ten pounds thinner and fretting over what to wear around the pool or at a concert. What's more, the garment industry continued to flourish while fashion shows remained as popular as ever and fashion magazines ballooned in size. Despite such indices of success, fashion was not what it once was: a source of moral suasion. No longer did Americans freight their clothing with virtue or trust it to set things right. For most postwar Americans, clothing had stopped serving as a compass whose coordinates registered national concern about what was appropriate and what was not. Only Catholics continued to associate clothing with the moral order. In 1953, for instance, the Reverend B. Kunkel of Bartelso, Illinois, launched a campaign to ensure that Catholic women had proper attire for formal occasions. He came up with the idea of identifying suitably modest prom and wedding dresses with a special tag—the "Marilyke tag," it was called—that bore a picture of the Virgin Mary and the text "Whatever Our Blessed Mother Approves." A number of metropolitan department stores and neighborhood dress shops lent their support to this venture (it would have been "business suicide" not to go along, one Linden, New Jersey, shopowner related), and within two years seventy-five thousand dresses had been tagged with the Marilyke seal of approval. For all its success within the American Catholic community, Reverend Kunkel's campaign spawned little interest outside it. No one picked up the ball. In fact, the church's reformist stance only highlighted the divide that separated the postwar generation from its predecessors.

The kind of soul searching that linked clothing with moral accountability had become a thing of the past along with the bustle and the big hat, the starched collar and the tasteful diamond. For a brief moment in the late 1960s, it looked as if fashion might once again generate an extended public discussion about the character and promise of America. Women put on miniskirts, took off their bras, and claimed the pants suit as their own; men let down their hair and wore bell-bottomed trousers festooned with flowers; and unisex, or "lookalikeness," as one pundit put it, was the word of the day. Everyone—rabbis, sociologists, columnists, and maître d's, who debated among themselves whether to admit women in pants to their restaurants—had something to say. But the discussion didn't go on for long. A last hurrah, it turned out to be as short-lived as the miniskirt.

In the end, a brand-new valuation of clothing took hold of the American imagination, one whose tenets held that getting dressed was a personal rather than a social form of expression, a way of heralding the individual rather than the community. As Rudi Gernreich, the designer of the topless bathing suit and the No-Bra bra, explained in 1969 when asked whether his creations signaled a weakening of America's moral fiber, "Morality is individual." If, earlier in the nation's history, getting dressed was a matter of fitting in, getting dressed in postwar America was increasingly a matter of standing out. Once tethered to the body politic, clothing now celebrated the self.

Notes

~

INTRODUCTION

PAGE

1. "cards of admission": Mary Brooks Picken, *The Secrets of Distinctive Dress* (Scranton, 1918), p. 4.

2. "merely a personal problem": Ida M. Tarbell, "The Great Problem of Clothes," *Ladies' Home Journal*, Apr. 1913, p. 26; May 1913, p. 26.

   "national taste in dress": Tarbell, May 1913, p. 26.

   "making of American women": "Is a Nation's Character Revealed in Its Dress?" *Craftsman*, Mar. 1914, p. 624; Picken, *Secrets of Distinctive Dress*, p. 49.

   "Mrs. Astorbilt": Anzia Yezierska, *Salome of the Tenements* (1923; Urbana, 1995), p. 27.

   "in itself culture": Abraham Cahan, *The Rise of David Levinsky* (1917; New York, 1960), p. 421.

3. "A whole book": Cahan, *Rise of David Levinsky*, pp. 110, 260.

"part of her birthright": Fannie Barrier Williams, "The Dress Burden," *National Association Notes*, May 1913, p. 8.

"bearing the burden": E. Azalia Hackley, *The Colored Girl Beautiful* (Kansas City, 1916), p. 31.

"best-dressed *average* woman": Cahan, *Rise of David Levinsky*, p. 444.

"every farm": "Shabby Clothes Not Due to Automobiles," *New York Times*, Jan. 13, 1924, sec. 2, p. 12.

4. "fairy godmother": "How the Mode Is Set and Upset," *Vogue*, Apr. 15, 1923, p. 37.

"guide to correct dress": Picken, "A Guide to Correct Dress for Business, Outing, and the Home—Spring Season," *Secrets of Distinctive Dress*, p. 82.

"democracy of beauty": This is the evocative title of chapter 5 of Yezierska's *Salome of the Tenements*.

With eager anticipation: "Dress-of-Month Plan Adopted by Macy's," *Business Week*, Aug. 26, 1931, p. 12; "To All of You Who Love Clothes . . . ," *Ladies' Home Journal*, Feb. 1933, p. 97; "Exposition to Have Temple of Fashion," *New York Times*, Oct. 21, 1925, p. 36; Annual Report, Alabama Polytechnic Institute Extension Services, 1927, p. 165.

5. "life of my forebears": Alice Morse Earle, *Two Centuries of Costume in America, 1620–1820* (New York, 1910), pp. 805, 806, 807.

CHAPTER ONE: À LA MODE

7. "No woman": "Extremely Simple to Make," *Ladies' Home Journal*, Apr. 1925, p. 81.

8. a headline: "Says Men Neglect Clothes to Keep Wives Well-Dressed," *New York Times*, Jan. 11, 1924, p. 19.

"Times have changed": "Colors for Men," *Saturday Evening Post*, Nov. 21, 1931, pp. 14, 15.

"His Royal Highness in Fashion": "Getting Percy Properly Drest," *Literary Digest*, Mar. 31, 1923, p. 424.

"social fact": Paul Nystrom, *Economics of Fashion* (New York, 1928), p. 35.

8   "to be out of fashion": Nystrom, *Economics of Fashion*, p. iii.

.   "First please the eye": Bertha A. Rich, "The Business Woman and the Powder Puff," *American Magazine*, Jan. 1918, p. 40.

        "buoy [his] courage": O. O. McIntyre, "Why I Like Snappy Clothes," *American Magazine*, Aug. 1924, p. 47.

9.   "cabalistic art": "Are Clothes Modern?" *Vogue*, Feb. 1, 1945, p. 172.

        "I could afford": Anne Aldworth, "Dress Making at Home," *Good Housekeeping*, Oct. 17, 1885, p. 15.

10.   "Secure the seam": Ibid.

        "Learning to cut": "Dress and Its Relation to Life," *Craftsman*, Nov. 1906, p. 271.

        "practice and art": "Is a Nation's Character Revealed in Its Dress?" *Craftsman*, Mar. 1914, p. 624.

11.   "vast army of mothers": Helen N. Packard, "Making Clothes for the Boys; with an Eye for Service, Economy and Comfort," *Good Housekeeping*, Sept. 5, 1885, p. 17.

        "To appear well-dressed": Emma Hooper, "To Dress Well on a Small Income," *Ladies' Home Journal*, Mar. 1901, p. 31; Feb. 1901, p. 30.

        Farm women: What follows is drawn from the records of the Alabama Cooperative Extension Service, RG 71, Auburn University Archives (hereafter ACES). I am profoundly indebted to Jane Przybysz, former curator of folklife at the McKissick Museum in Columbia, S.C., for her extraordinary generosity in sharing this material with me.

        "clothing specialists": "Clothing Demonstrations, 1936–37," in Dorothy Dean, Annual Report of Extension Clothing and Handicraft, 1936–37, n.p., ACES.

        "Next to poultry": Annual Report of State Home Demonstration Agent, 1923, p. 14, ACES.

12.   "country woman self respect": Report of Clothing Specialist, Josephine F. Eddy, Nov. 1, 1922–Nov. 1, 1923, p. 5, ACES.

        "Good taste in renovation": Mary Shaw Gilliam, Annual Report, South Carolina Extension Service, 1935, p. 13, Clemson University Special Collections.

        Ingenuity, skill, and pedagogy: The following draws on material culled from "Home Demonstration [Report]," South Carolina Extension Service, 1933, p. 59, Clemson University Special Collections.

12. "humble flour and food sack": Dorothy Dean, Annual Report, Extension Service, Alabama Polytechnic Institute, 1932, p. 28, ACES.

   several Alabama women: See, for example, Mrs. M. E. Bishop, "Sack Work—41 Pieces Cost $1.30," in Dean, Annual Report, Extension Service, Alabama Polytechnic Institute, 1929–30, p. 59; Bess Fleming, "Women Make Useful Articles from Sacks," n.d., n.p., appended to Dean, Annual Report, Extension Service, Alabama Polytechnic Institute, 1929–30.

14. "done by fairy fingers": Sara Josepha Hale of *Godey's Lady's Book*, cited in Nancy Page Fernandez, "Innovations in Home Dressing and the Popularization of Stylish Dress," *Journal of American Culture* 17, no. 3 (1994), p. 29.

   "none but students": Catherine Broughton, *Suggestions for Dressmakers* (New York, 1896), p. 7.

   "yankee ingenuity": Packard, "Making Clothes for the Boys."

   "bitter, bitter tears": Aldworth, "Dress Making at Home."

   "they try to sew": Hooper, "To Dress Well on a Small Income," Mar. 1901, p. 31.

15. "little knee pants": Packard, "Making Clothes for the Boys."

   "become food for . . . moths": Ibid.

   "busy in the interest": "Report of the National Committee on Cooperation," *Nineteenth Annual Report, National Federation of Temple Sisterhoods*, 1932, p. 100.

16. thrift shops: Publications of women's philanthropic organizations like the National Council of Jewish Women's *News Letter* and its *Council Woman* magazine are filled with details about thrift shops and their role in philanthropic culture.

   "After an apprenticeship": Fanchon W. Schwager, "Two-Way Thrift," *Council Woman*, Mar.–Apr. 1941, p. 11.

   "It means dignity": *Council Woman*, Oct. 1953, p. 12.

   "I buy!": Donald Paneth, "I Cash Clothes!" *Commentary*, June 1950, pp. 556–57.

18. "This is the sign": "Send for the 'Waste Bag,'" *American Hebrew*, May 12, 1916, p. 16.

"I like to walk": Paneth, "I Cash Clothes!" p. 557.

19. "the bag of the rag-picker": Frederick Boyd Stevenson, "At the Secondhand Clothes Mart: In Bayard Street, New York, One Buys and Sells without Fear and without Reproach," *Harper's Weekly*, Mar. 25, 1911, p. 24.

$3 million a year: What follows is drawn from Aaron Kosofsky, "Second-Hand Clothing—Who Sells It and Who Buys It," *American Magazine*, Dec. 1921, pp. 20–21, 122–24.

"It is no light achievement": "Old-Clothes Sensation," *Atlantic Monthly*, July 1915, pp. 139–40.

Fanny Brice: "Second Hand Rose," music composed by James F. Hanley; words by Grant Clarke. Original copyright held by Shapiro, Bernstein & Co., 1921. The song was to be sung "Tempo di Fox Trot."

20. "deep sense of satisfaction": Henrietta Flack, Introduction to Sylvia K. Mager, *A Complete Guide to Home Sewing* (New York, 1960), p. x.

ready-to-wear industry: Irwin Franklyn, "On a Firm Foundation," ms., Jan. 29, 1942, p. 6, WPA, Jews of New York, Jews in Industry, Microfilm Reel 159, New York City Municipal Archives. See also Nancy Green, *Ready-to-Wear, Ready-to-Work* (Durham, 1997).

An intricate network: *National Jeweler*, Dec. 1925, p. 23; Virginia Pope, "Behind the Easter Parade of Fashion," *New York Times Magazine*, Apr. 21, 1935, p. 8.

22. pretty clothes: "Farm Girls and Pretty Clothes," *New York Times*, Dec. 15, 1926, p. 26.

Fifth Avenue emporium: Advertisements for Stern and B. Altman appear in *The Year Book, New York Section, National Council of Jewish Women*, 1925–26, frontispiece and pp. 2, 20, respectively.

In Los Angeles: Nystrom, *Economics of Fashion*, pp. 479–80.

something for everyone: "Time to Enjoy the Bathing Suit," *American Hebrew*, May 26, 1916, p. 98; "Macy's New Marwood Fashions," *New York Times*, Mar. 24, 1929, p. 11; "Business-Like Apparel for the Business Woman—Another New Service at Greater Macy's," *New York Times*, Oct. 16, 1924, p. 7; Ruth Glazer, "West Bronx: Food, Shelter, Clothing," *Commentary*, June 1949, p. 583.

22. Even casual housedresses: What follows is drawn from Charles Lane Cullen, "It's All Right to Be a Wife If You Don't Look Like One," *American Magazine*, Nov. 1927, pp. 18, 76, 82.

23. ready-made clothing reflected: "What Is Kamp-it?" in "Serviceable Clothing for Life in the Open," Utica-Duxbak Corporation, Utica, n.d., p. 16, Collection of the Adirondack Museum, Blue Mountain Lake, New York; "New Styles for Women Automobilists," *Scientific American Supplement*, Mar. 12, 1904, p. 23576; "The 'Lenox Ulster,'" in "The Red Gods Call!" Abercrombie & Fitch, New York, 1913, p. 8, Collection of the Adirondack Museum, Blue Mountain Lake, New York. I would like to thank Jerold Pepper, librarian of the Adirondack Museum, for generously sharing this material with me.

"very alert": Frances Maule, *She Strives to Conquer: Business Behavior, Opportunities and Job Requirements for Women* (New York, 1936), pp. 128–29.

And for a night: Grace Corson, "Screen Inspired Readymades Selected for Photoplay Readers," *Photoplay*, May 1925, pp. 49–53; "Hollywood Fashions," *Photoplay*, Oct. 1932, p. 121; "Cinema Fashions," *Fortune*, Jan. 1937, pp. 38, 44; Lillian Churchill, "Modes à la Movies," *New York Times Magazine*, Jan. 7, 1940, p. 9; Margaret Case Harriman, "Very Terrific, Very Divine: A Profile of Nettie Rosenstein," *New Yorker*, Oct. 19, 1940, p. 28.

"purely American pleasure": Harriman, "Very Terrific, Very Divine." See also Abraham Cahan, *The Rise of David Levinsky* (1917; New York, 1960), p. 443, and Green, *Ready-to-Wear, Ready-to-Work*, pp. 44–73.

24. "Cinderella clothes": Anzia Yezierska, *Salome of the Tenements* (1923; Urbana, 1995), p. 8.

25. "just like an American": Quoted in Barbara Schreier, *Becoming*

American Women: Clothing and the Jewish Immigrant Experience, 1880–1920 (Chicago, 1994), p. 56.

25. "a great deal of joy": Rose Gallup Cohen, *Out of the Shadow* (New York, 1918), p. 169.

"as American as turning on": "Rules for Clothes," *Vogue,* Feb. 1, 1945, p. 144.

In the South: Dean, Annual Report of Extension Work in Clothing and Handicraft, 1929, p. 73, ACES; "Sack-Work—Dale County," Dean, Annual Report, Extension Service, Alabama Polytechnic Institute, 1929–30, p. 55, ACES.

"Ten-cent store clerks": Robert S. Lynd and Helen Merrell Lynd, *Middletown: A Study in Contemporary American Culture* (New York, 1929), p. 82.

Women's groups: "40th Anniversary Convention Celebrated," *Hadassah Newsletter,* Nov. 1951, p. 6; "Convention Report," *Hadassah Newsletter,* Nov. 1953, p. 8. See also Shane White and Graham White, *Stylin': African American Expressive Culture from Its Beginnings to the Zoot Suit* (Ithaca, 1998), pp. 208–15, esp. p. 211.

Before long: Later still, the fashion show made itself at home on television. "TV makes the illustration of clothes come to life," wrote Irwin A. Shane, publisher of the *Televiser,* keen on exploiting an affinity between the two. "Suppose you picked up a copy of *Harper's Bazaar* and suddenly the very attractive model in the ad for Formfit Brassieres came to life. I'm sure you'd experience quite a lift" ("Television for Retailers," *Televiser,* Fall 1944, p. 35).

27. "And the show is on": Franklyn, "On a Firm Foundation," pp. 1, 4.

Fur Fashion Show: "Fur Fashion Show," *New York Times,* Apr. 27, 1922, p. 17.

"pink mink": *Council Woman,* Feb. 1955, p. 12.

"Castaway Cavalcade": *Council Woman,* Winter 1947, p. 16.

28. "smart enough": "Fund Raising," National Council of Jewish Women, *News Letter,* Spring 1937, p. 57.

"dress revue": Dean, Annual Report, Extension Service, Alabama Polytechnic Institute, 1932, pp. 27ff.

28. "travelling costume contest": "The Girls' Travelling Costume Team," in Dean, Annual Report of Extension Work in Clothing and Handicraft, 1929, pp. 72–75.

29. Henry County: "Program—Henry County Clothing Rally," in Dean, Annual Report of Extension Work in Clothing and Handicraft, 1929, pp. 61–62.

"buymanship": "Clothing Demonstrations, 1936–37," n.p.

"Teachers are everywhere": Zella E. Bigelow, "Suggestions for a Demonstration of the Selection of Clothing," *Journal of Home Economics*, Feb. 1920, pp. 69, 71.

30. "clothing contest": Lillian Peek, "Girls' Clothing Contests," *Journal of Home Economics*, Feb. 1926, pp. 74, 78.

"suitability, durability": Bigelow, "Suggestions," p. 69.

score cards: U.S. Department of Agriculture, "Score Cards for Judging Clothing Selection and Construction," Miscellaneous Circular No. 90, 1927, p. 2.

31. "great topics": "Fashion and the Development of Women," *Craftsman*, Feb. 1914, p. 505.

"A president": "The Tyranny of Fashion," *Independent*, Mar. 2, 1905, p. 510.

Some early-twentieth-century Americans: "Shirt-Waists from a Craftsman's Point of View," *Craftsman*, Feb. 1907, p. 648; "Dame Fashion's Thumb," *Current Literature*, Feb. 1902, p. 229.

"hurried": Mary Brooks Picken, *The Secrets of Distinctive Dress* (Scranton, 1918), p. 191.

"ungraceful, foolish and shoddy": "Is a Nation's Character Revealed in Its Dress?" p. 624.

"ninety percent freak": Emily Post, *Etiquette: The Blue Book of Social Usage* (New York, 1922), p. 694. Eventually, Post was to change her mind. Writing in 1936, she conceded that matters had greatly improved: "It is only fair to American tailors to acknowledge that such amazing improvement has been made in the cut and finish of ready-to-wear clothes" (*Etiquette* [New York, 1936], p. 597).

"no works of art": Florence B. Rose, "One Should Keep Up Regarding Clothes in the Same Manner as One Keeps Up with the Times," *American Weekly Jewish News*, Apr. 19, 1918, p. 16.

32. "stylish stout": Frances Donovan, *The Saleslady* (Chicago, 1929), p. 51.

Retailers also added: "Sizes Askew on Women's Clothing," *New York Times*, Jan. 17, 1926, sec. 2, p. 21. On sizing, see also Nystrom, "Standardization of Sizes and Types of Apparel," *Economics of Fashion*, pp. 452–81.

"disease-breeding garments": Nancy Tomes, *The Gospel of Germs: Men, Women and the Microbe in American Life* (Cambridge, 1998), p. 218.

33. "Disaster seems": "Fashion and the Development of Women," p. 506; Fannie Barrier Williams, "The Dress Burden," *National Association Notes*, May 1913, p. 8.

"Crops may fail": Quoted in "Must Women Go Back to Tripping Over Their Trains?" *Literary Digest*, Nov. 16, 1929, p. 39.

"god of novelty": "Paris Fashions and American Women," *Craftsman*, Jan. 1910, p. 466; Fannie Hurst, "Let's Not Wear Them!" *New Republic*, Oct. 30, 1929, p. 294.

"good education": "Fashion and the Development of Women," p. 506.

"Our minds": Quoted in *American Hebrew*, July 17, 1925, p. 328.

"automatically as an instantaneous": "Now Coats of Many Colors," *New York Times*, Sept. 24, 1926, p. 32.

34. "real self that is you": "By Their Dress Shall You Know Them," *American Weekly Jewish News*, Dec. 20, 1918, p. 704.

"To be fashionable": Picken, *Secrets of Distinctive Dress*, p. 7.

"A star's life": "Setting Styles through the Stars," *Ladies' Home Journal*, Feb. 1933, p. 10.

35. "slim purse": *Vogue*, May 1, 1923, p. 41.

to "see the world": Ibid.; "Smart Fashions for Limited Incomes," *Vogue*, May 15, 1923, pp. 60–65.

"so cleverly": *Vogue*, May 1, 1923, p. 41.

"alert, efficient": Maule, *She Strives to Conquer*, pp. 127, 128, 136.

"circumstantially denied": *Hebrew Standard*, Apr. 5, 1907, p. 20.

37. "The woman who worships": Williams, "Dress Burden," p. 9.

37. "awakens the most revolting": "A Word in Due Season," *American Hebrew,* Sept. 29, 1911, p. 677.

"great stress": Viola Paradise, "The Jewish Immigrant Girl in Chicago," *Survey,* Sept. 6, 1913, p. 704.

Young African American women: E. Azalia Hackley, *The Colored Girl Beautiful* (Kansas City, 1916), pp. 121, 74, 75.

38. "They imitate": Quoted in Schreier, *Becoming American Women,* p. 107.

39. "in danger of taking": Paradise, "Jewish Immigrant Girl," p. 704.

"fine dressing": Williams, "Dress Burden," p. 9.

"Perhaps at no time": Paradise, "Jewish Immigrant Girl," p. 704.

"good taste in dress": Lana Bishop, "Bettering of Taste in Dress and Home Furnishing through Domestic Art," *Journal of Home Economics,* June 1909, p. 282.

"effeminate employments": *Report of the Louis Down-Town Sabbath and Daily School, October 1886–June 1887,* p. 37; "Medical Report," *Annual Report, Hebrew Technical School for Girls,* 1907, pp. 11, 42.

40. "you would think": Cited in Jenna Weissman Joselit, *Aspiring Women* (New York, 1996), p. 27.

"principles of color selection": "Color in Clothing Courses for Negro Children," *Journal of Home Economics,* May 1926, p. 270.

Teresa Staats: Ibid.

W. E. B. Du Bois: W. E. B. Du Bois, "Diuturni Silenti," in *The Education of Black People: Ten Critiques, 1906–1960,* ed. Herbert Aptheker (Amherst, 1973), pp. 53ff. A generation later, in a curious twist of events, the African American's "flair for color" was celebrated rather than condemned. In 1941, *Life* reported that blacks in the South were now being seen as a "source of fashion inspiration." American fashion designers like Doris Lee, an "imaginative artist who finds hidden beauty in simple scenes and people," the magazine related, came up with a winter resort line for Marshall Field & Company that took its stylistic cue from the brightly colored and inventively shaped clothing worn by the African American residents of Beaufort, South Carolina ("Doris

Lee Offers the Southern Negro as a Source of Fashion Inspiration," *Life,* Dec. 8, 1941, pp. 96–97).

40. Properly channeled: Hackley, *Colored Girl Beautiful,* pp. 72, 137, 48.

41. A Pledge for the American Woman: Picken, *Secrets of Distinctive Dress,* p. 215.

CHAPTER TWO: DOWN WITH THE CORSET AND UP WITH THE HEMLINE!

43. "feminine personality": Frances R. Donovan, *The Saleslady* (Chicago, 1929), p. 46.

woman's "birthright": Edward Bok, "A Woman's Questions," *Ladies' Home Journal,* Apr. 1901, p. 16.

44. "flowing outline": C. H. Crandall, "What Men Think of Women's Dress," *North American Review,* Aug. 1895, p. 252.

"beauty of a free personality": Louis Fraina, quoted in Christine Stansell, *American Moderns: Bohemian New York and the Creation of a New Century* (New York, 2000), p. 233.

"shin-swaddling flounces": "Must Women Go Back to Tripping Over Their Trains?" *Literary Digest,* Nov. 16, 1929, p. 39.

"as a mere rotary ball": Frances Willard, quoted in Frances E. Russell, "A Brief Survey of the American Dress Reform Movements of the Past, with Views of Representative Women," *Arena,* Aug. 1892, p. 339.

46. "whalebone thralldom": "Corset versus Corset-Waist," *American Jewess,* Dec. 1895, p. 171.

"We only wore it": Quoted in Russell, "Brief Survey," p. 327.

"question of American costume": What follows, including Croly's comments, is drawn from Russell, "Brief Survey," p. 331.

"calculable injury": Elizabeth Stuart Phelps, *What to Wear,* quoted in Russell, "Brief Survey," p. 333.

"dress-protestants": Helen Ecob, *The Well-Dressed Woman: A Study in the Practical Application to Dress of the Laws of Health, Art and Morals* (New York, 1892), p. 129.

"antisepticonsciousness": William W. Bauer, "Antisepticonscious

America," *American Mercury*, July 1933, pp. 323–26. See also Nancy Tomes, *The Gospel of Germs* (Cambridge, 1998).

47. "The streets": "Septic Skirts," *Scientific American*, Aug. 18, 1900, p. 108.

several cigar ends: Viscountess F. W. Harberton, "How It Is We Get On No Faster," Symposium on Women's Dress, *Arena*, Oct. 1892, p. 622.

"If men were compelled": "Man's Most Vulgar Habit," *Ladies' Home Journal*, May 1897, p. 14.

49. "hobbling, crippling impediment": "Osteopaths Favor 'Freedom' in Dress," *New York Times*, Mar. 24, 1929, p. 19.

Rainy Daisies: "Rainy Day Club Marks 25th Year," *New York Times*, Nov. 6, 1922, sec. 2, p. 11.

"Just four inches": "Rainy Daisies Triumph," *New York Times*, Oct. 30, 1921, sec. 7, p. 10.

"correct," "rational": Mrs. Jenness Miller, "Artistic and Sensible Dress," Symposium on Women's Dress, *Arena*, Sept. 1892, p. 495.

"The corset-curse": Ecob, *Well-Dressed Woman*, pp. 122, 87, 82, 238.

50. "mostly autobiographical": See, for example, Grace Greenwood, "On Woman's Dress—Mostly Autobiographical," Symposium on Women's Dress, *Arena*, Oct. 1892, pp. 631–34.

"manometer": Robert L. Dickinson, "The Corset: Questions of Pressure and Displacement," *New York Medical Journal*, Nov. 5, 1887, pp. 507–16.

51. "niggardly waists": Quoted in Ecob, *Well-Dressed Woman*, pp. 28–29.

"no use for fashion-plates": Ecob, *Well-Dressed Woman*, pp. 216, 143, and ch. 10, "Practical Suggestions."

"unburdensome and unshackling": Greenwood, "On Woman's Dress" p. 634.

"dirt-escapable": Ecob, *Well-Dressed Woman*, p. 144.

"with the ancient instruments": Greenwood, "On Woman's Dress," p. 634.

"lingering penchant": Ecob, *Well-Dressed Woman*, pp. 133, 132, 131, 135–37.

53. "inverted cone": Ecob, *Well-Dressed Woman*, p. 189.

"charming gown": Greenwood, "On Woman's Dress," p. 634.

"button that buttoned": Ecob, *Well-Dressed Woman*, p. 220.

53. "I am very stout": Ecob anticipated—and answered—many of her readers' objections. See pp. 140–41.

"Off with the corsets": "Dress in the Kitchen," *American Jewess*, May 1895, p. 90.

55. "wheelwomen": B. O. Flower, "The Next Forward Step for Women," Symposium on Women's Dress, *Arena*, Oct. 1892, p. 641; "Emperor William and the 'New Woman,' " *American Jewess*, Jan. 1896, p. 198.

Octavia Bates: Octavia Bates, "The Dress of College Women from a College Woman's Outlook," Symposium on Women's Dress, *Arena*, Oct. 1892, pp. 625–27.

"What if ": Frances E. Russell, "Lines of Beauty," Symposium on Women's Dress, *Arena*, Sept. 1892, p. 503.

"While the men": "Rainy Daisies Triumph," p. 10.

"A short-skirted woman": "A Plea for Long Skirts," *Harper's Bazaar*, Dec. 8, 1900, p. 2066.

56. "corset-wearing nation": "Corsets for Women Workers," *Literary Digest*, July 13, 1918, p. 22. I'd like to thank my student Ayelet Cohen for bringing this reference to my attention.

"artless announcement": "Plea for Long Skirts," p. 2066.

"a tendency to reveal": "Editor's Desk," *American Jewess*, July 1895, p. 195.

"A woman in bloomers": "To Honor Mrs. Amelia Bloomer," *American Jewess*, Nov. 1895, p. 107. Dress reformers happened to be extremely sensitive to the charge that they knowingly sacrificed beauty for comfort. Sensible clothing was a "perpetual violation of my love of the beautiful," conceded Elizabeth Smith Miller, a member of the National Council of Women's Committee on Dress, noting that, as her aesthetic sense "gained ascendancy," she had no choice but to put away her rational dress. See Elizabeth Smith Miller, "Reflections on Women's Dress and the Record of a Personal Experience," Symposium on Women's Dress, *Arena*, Sept. 1892, p. 494.

57. "We must look": Dr. Dudley A. Sargent, "Hygiene, Dress and Dress Reform," *Journal of Home Economics*, June 1910, p. 298.

57. "The majority of women": Harberton, "How It Is We Get On No Faster," p. 624.

"affectation of queer": Bok, "Woman's Questions," p. 16.

"hoydenish": "Plea for Long Skirts," p. 2066.

"mannish middle-aged": Sargent, "Hygiene, Dress and Dress Reform," p. 305.

"vision of short hair": Ibid.

58. "woman's mission": "The Side That's Next the Sun," *Ladies' Home Journal*, May 1898, p. 14.

"trials": "Madame La Mode," *American Jewess*, May 1896, p. 432; "Will the Fashion Last?" *New York Times*, Sept. 4, 1910, p. 8; "Rainy Daisies Triumph," p. 10.

59. "new era of undressing": Bruce Bliven, "Flapper Jane," *New Republic*, Sept. 9, 1925, p. 67.

"two-ounce underthings": Ibid.

"clothes chronicle": Fannie Hurst, "Let's Not Wear Them!" *New Republic*, Oct. 30, 1929, p. 294.

60. "dead as the dodo's grandfather": Bliven, "Flapper Jane," p. 65.

"rode low": Hurst, "Let's Not Wear Them!" p. 294.

"Sportelette": "Woman's Friend, the Corset," *Literary Digest*, Nov. 5, 1921, p. 20.

"do more for your figure": Advertisement for H. W. Gossard corsets, *Ladies' Home Journal*, Jan. 1924, p. 117.

"We choose them": "We Choose Them Slim and Short for Summer," *Ladies' Home Journal*, Feb. 1925, p. 60.

"Whatever fashion": "Large Women at Their Worst and Best," *Ladies' Home Journal*, Apr. 1925, p. 72; Donovan, *Saleslady*, p. 51.

"Being smartly": "Attractive Frocks Seen in and after Office Hours," *Ladies' Home Journal*, Jan. 1924, p. 57; "Every Month— Clothes for the Business Woman to Wear in and out of the Office," *Ladies' Home Journal*, Apr. 1924, pp. 60–61.

"Ten years ago": "Mothers Wear Same Styles as Daughters 'N' Same Sizes, Too," *Chicago Tribune*, n.d., cited in Donovan, *Saleslady*, pp. 58–59.

61. "regiment": Mildred Adams, "Revolt Rumbles in the Fashion World," *New York Times,* Oct. 27, 1929, sec. 5, p. 4.

"We can now dodge": "New Fashions," *American Hebrew,* Mar. 26, 1915, p. 605.

62. "express a modern": Ibid.

"be taken out": Quoted in "Rainy Daisies Triumph."

"never to speak": "Sets Out to Reform Dress and Customs," *New York Times,* May 18, 1921, p. 36; *New York Times,* Mar. 22, 1922, p. 17.

"Was that cruelty?": *New York Times,* Dec. 25, 1928, p. 36.

63. "swing the pendulum": Ellery Rand, "Mrs. Henderson Crusades for Modesty," *New York Times,* Jan. 31, 1926, sec. 8, p. 4.

"We must do something": "Wants School Girls to Hide Their Knees," *New York Times,* Jan. 27, 1922, p. 10.

"Girls, between 15 and 25": "Blames Flimsy Modern Dress for Increase in Tuberculosis," *New York Times,* Aug. 8, 1927, p. 1. Some doctors took the opposite tack, lauding short skirts for the way they enabled "ultra-violet rays from the sun" to enter the body. See, for example, "Osteopaths Favor 'Freedom' in Dress."

"assumption that such exposures": "She Speaks with No Authority," *New York Times,* Dec. 27, 1921, p. 12. See also Jeannette Throckmorten, "Fashions as Affecting Public Health," *American Journal of Public Health,* Nov. 1918, pp. 817–20.

As the need for fabric: Bliven, "Flapper Jane," p. 65; Paul Nystrom, *Economics of Fashion* (New York, 1928), p. 434.

"renaissance of the long skirt": "Urges Long Skirts for Cotton Relief," *New York Times,* May 14, 1927, p. 19; "Textile Mills See Aid in Long Easter Frocks," *New York Times,* Apr. 1, 1929, p. 3.

"Of all the absurd": Letter to the Editor, *New York Times,* May 18, 1927, p. 24.

64. "straight-backed": "Society Women Hit at Immodest Dress," *New York Times,* Dec. 27, 1925, p. 14.

Women like her: Cigarette smoking was also to be avoided, at all costs. Like "vulgar fashions," it could only lead to "physical bankruptcy" ("Society Women Hit at Immodest Dress," p. 14;

"A New Crusade for Longer Skirts," *Literary Digest,* Jan. 16, 1926, p. 31).

64. "It really is amazing": Rand, "Mrs. Henderson Crusades for Modesty," pp. 4, 9.

America's religious leaders: "Rome Orders Decent Dress," *New York Times,* Oct. 1, 1925, p. 6; *New York Times,* Mar. 1, 1927, p. 16; "Fixes Length of Skirt," *New York Times,* Jan. 31, 1922, p. 19.

65. Religious prescriptive literature: See, for example, Rev. Francis X. Lasance, ed., *The Catholic Girl's Guide* (New York, 1906), p. 183; Sue Blakely, *Appeal to Christian Young Women* (Boston, 1870), p. 39.

"love of finery": Rabbi Israel Levinthal, "Style," Dec. 29, 1916, Levinthal Collection, Ratner Center for the Study of Conservative Judaism, Jewish Theological Seminary of America, New York.

"All the precepts": "Paris Gibes at Moral Gown," *New York Times,* Feb. 17, 1921, p. 6.

new oratorical heights: What follows is drawn from "Dr. Wise Attacks Fashion's Follies," *New York Times,* Jan. 2, 1922, p. 22.

66. "Mary's Little Skirt": *New York Times,* June 27, 1921, p. 13.

"strenuous": "Italy to Set Own Style," *New York Times,* July 19, 1925, sec. 2, p. 7; "Pope's Admonition Brings Change in Italian Dress," *New York Times,* Sept. 6, 1925, sec. 7, p. 11.

"Christ Himself": *New York Times,* Feb. 17, 1929, sec. 3, p. 3; "Catholic Women Bar Immodest Garb," *New York Times,* Dec. 3, 1925, p. 27.

"consistent Catholic women": *Catholic Telegraph,* cited in "The Pope's Appeal to Men to Reform Women's Dress," *Literary Digest,* Jan. 29, 1927, p. 57.

"I like to go": Robert S. Lynd and Helen Merrell Lynd, *Middletown: A Study in Contemporary American Culture* (New York, 1929), p. 361.

"Religion hasn't anything": Emily Solis-Cohen, "The Jewish Girl's Thoughts on Jewish Life," *United Synagogue Recorder,* Oct. 1925, p. 10.

Dressed in their best: Leah Morton, *I Am a Woman—and a Jew* (New York, 1926), p. 238.

"It may perchance": Mary Brooks Picken, *The Secrets of Distinctive Dress* (Scranton, 1918), p. 190.

67. "all truly Catholic": "Modesty in Dress," *Homiletic and Pastoral Review,* July 1931, p. 1100; "Lady Armstrong for Modest Dress," *New York Times,* Dec. 6, 1925, p. 28.

"It is so easy": Warfield Webb, "Good Example in Dress," *Ave Maria,* Mar. 7, 1936, p. 307.

"war against immodest dress": "Church Bars Scant Dress," *New York Times,* Sept. 5, 1925, p. 11.

"Fathers, sons and husbands": *New York Times,* Mar. 10, 1927, p. 1. See also Dec. 14, 1926, p. 1.

"Skirts are not": "Rolled Stockings Barred by College," *New York Times,* Jan. 5, 1927, p. 6.

Leaving nothing to chance: Janet Collier, Lorraine Fuhrmann, and Kathleen Joyce, personal communication. See also "Parents, Sisters and School-Clothes," *Ave Maria,* Sept. 12, 1955, pp. 8–11.

"Wear longer skirts": *New York Times,* Apr. 7, 1926, p. 2.

68. "back to normalcy drive": "Fixes Length of Skirts," p. 19.

"must not be higher": "Regulates Dress for Bridal Parties," *New York Times,* Dec. 4, 1921, p. 4.

"The dictates of fashion": *Catholic Citizen,* cited in "Pope's Appeal to Men," p. 57.

"almost universal disregard": "Rolled Stockings Barred by College," p. 6.

"We have heard": "Discretion Necessary in Preaching against Immodest Dress," *Homiletic and Pastoral Review,* Apr. 1930, p. 751.

"With all the vigor": Ibid.

69. "edicts": "Catholic Women Favor World Peace," *New York Times,* Nov. 19, 1925, p. 24.

First, it cautioned: "Massachusetts Church Bars Women Wearing Short Skirts," *New York Times,* Mar. 29, 1921, p. 19.

"twelve rules of dress": "Instruction concerning Indecent Dress of

Women," *Homiletic and Pastoral Review*, Apr. 1930, pp. 757–59; "Full Text of Rules by Pope on Dress," *New York Times*, Feb. 7, 1930, p. 5.

69. Some Jews: "Jews Commend Catholic Ban on Immodest Garb," *New York Evening World*, Oct. 27, 1925, p. 21; "Want Modest Garb for Jewish Women," *New York Times*, Oct. 27, 1925, p. 15.

"with disfavor upon": The full text of the resolution can be found in Herbert S. Goldstein, "A Year of Orthodoxy," *Jewish Forum*, Dec. 1925, p. 563; "Church Decrees on Women's Dress," *Literary Digest*, Nov. 21, 1925, p. 32.

70. "A church cannot": "Want Modest Garb," p. 15; "Church Decrees," p. 32.

"powerful forces": "Well-Dressed Women," *New York Times*, Oct. 28, 1925, p. 24.

71. "From morning to night": "Vogue's-Eye View of the Mode," *Vogue*, Oct. 15, 1927, p. 61.

"feminine in the most": Adams, "Revolt Rumbles," p. 4.

"telescope the years": Ibid.

"Had the life": "Dress Designer as a World Force," *New York Times*, Oct. 20, 1927, p. 28.

"Stylish women": "Poiret Backs Pope," *New York Times*, Aug. 17, 1928, p. 6.

"Knees have withdrawn": *Newark Evening News*, quoted in "Must Women Go Back to Tripping," p. 49.

"Not on your life": Adams, "Revolt Rumbles," p. 5; "Must Women Go Back to Tripping," p. 39.

A poll conducted: "Seventy Percent of Hunter Girls Rebel at Long Skirts," *New York Times*, Nov. 25, 1929, p. 27.

72. "freedom of their limbs": "Women Renew Fight against Short Skirts," *New York Times*, Sept. 30, 1922, p. 15; Adams, "Revolt Rumbles," p. 5.

"Here is one": Hurst, "Let's Not Wear Them!" p. 294.

73. Other women penned: Adams, "Revolt Rumbles," p. 5; Ruth MacIntire Dadourian, "Correspondence: Women and the New Style," *New Republic*, Dec. 18, 1929, p. 101.

"the long and the short": "Talks Fail to Fix Length of Skirts," *New York Times*, Dec. 13, 1929, p. 36.

"lift themselves out": Ibid.

CHAPTER THREE: THE MARK OF A GENTLEMAN

75. "The sex with which": Frederick Lewis Allen, "Fall Fashions for Men," *Forum*, Nov. 1926, p. 661.

"inflexible as the laws": "Modes and the Man," *Living Age*, Apr. 19, 1913, p. 189.

76. "The movement of men's fashions": Frederick Lewis Allen, *Only Yesterday: An Informal History of the Nineteen-Twenties* (New York, 1931), p. 2.

"standard masculine": Anne Hollander, *Sex and Suits* (New York, 1994), p. 3.

"When men wore satins": "Now Coats of Many Colors," *New York Times*, Sept. 24, 1926, p. 32.

"pleasure of being well-dressed": "Begin Drive to Teach Men How to Dress—Clothiers Are Informed That Male Americans Do Not Buy Enough Raiment," *New York Times*, Sept. 10, 1926, p. 26.

"to occasion raucous mirth": "Getting Percy Properly Drest," *Literary Digest*, Mar. 31, 1923, p. 44.

77. "dressing badly": Elizabeth Hawes, *Men Can Take It* (New York, 1939), p. 66.

From their vantage point: See, for example, Elias Tobenkin, *God of Might* (New York, 1925), p. 103.

"pansies": Hawes, *Men Can Take It*, p. 66.

"If we are honest": O. O. McIntyre, "Why I Like Snappy Clothes," *American Magazine*, Aug. 1924, p. 47.

Rabbi Alexander Kohut: Rebekah Kohut, *As I Know Them: Some Jews and a Few Gentiles* (Garden City, 1929), p. 171.

78. Laymen like Mr. Wolfson: S. N. Behrman, "Mr. Wolfson's Stained-Glass Window," *The Worcester Account* (New York, 1954), pp. 197–98.

"I really *enjoy*": McIntyre, "Why I Like Snappy Clothes," p. 47.

78. "sartorial metamorphosis": Anonymous, "What Good Clothes Did for Me," *American Magazine*, Feb. 1919, pp. 94–100.

79. "ten commandments": "Fashion's Edicts Ban 'Jazz' Attire for Men," *New York Times*, Sept. 22, 1926, p. 27.

"cheerfully but soberly": "The Offense of the Colored Shirt," *Ladies' Home Journal*, June 1897, p. 14; The Major of To-day [pseud.], *Clothes and the Man: Hints on the Wearing and Caring of Clothes* (New York, 1900), p. 142.

"badge of the man": Frances Anne Allen, "The Vestments of the Male," *American Mercury*, June 1928, p. 215.

"luridly colored": "The Offense of the Colored Shirt."

"correct dress chart": See, for example, "Correct Dress Chart for Winter, 1909," in Frederick Taylor Frazer, "What's What in Men's Dress," *Ladies' Home Journal*, Jan. 1909, p. 36.

80. "What man in his senses": *Clothes and the Man*, p. 81.

"contrivances for keeping trousers": "What Good Clothes Did for Me," p. 96; *Clothes and the Man*, p. 90.

81. "a pair of trousers": *Clothes and the Man*, p. 89.

"no respectable man": *Clothes and the Man*, pp. 100–01.

"A man wants": Watson G. Clark, "What a Dyer and Cleaner Knows about You and Your Clothes," *American Magazine*, July 1924, p. 133.

82. "gospel of civility": E. M. Woods, Preface, *The Negro in Etiquette: A Novelty* (St. Louis, 1899); see also ch. 9, "The Freedman's Progress in Refinement, Compared with That of Thirty-three Years Ago," especially pp. 73–74.

"abate, by jot or tittle": Mrs. M. F. Armstrong, *Habits and Manners. Revised Edition. Adapted to General Use* (Hampton, 1888), pp. 54, 78, 80.

83. "raising the social": Woods, Preface, *Negro in Etiquette*.

"foppish fellow": Woods, *Negro in Etiquette*, pp. 93, 58, 60, 34–36.

Every Sunday: Kathleen Adams, cited in Shane White and Graham White, *Stylin': African American Expressive Culture from Its Beginnings to the Zoot Suit* (Ithaca, 1998), p. 164.

"at least one Sunday suit": Quoted in White and White, *Stylin'*, p. 163.

83. "good, well cared for": White and White, *Stylin'*, p. 174.

84. "keen eye": Hutchins Hapgood, *The Spirit of the Ghetto* (New York, 1902), p. 33.

85. "artistic taste": *New York Tribune,* Aug. 26, 1900, quoted in Allon Schoener, ed., *Portal to America* (New York, 1967), pp. 121–22.

    "genteel American": Abraham Cahan, *The Rise of David Levinsky* (1917; New York, 1960), pp. 260, 95.

    "several suits": Tobenkin, *God of Might,* pp. 103–04.

    "all manner of boys' clothing": Samuel Chotzinoff, *A Lost Paradise: Early Reminiscences* (New York, 1955), pp. 63, 68.

    "we have to love": "His Clothes—As Seen by Her: The Candid Opinions of Some Half a Hundred Young Women on the Momentous Subject of Male Attire," *Good Housekeeping,* July 1909, p. 15.

87. commented the *New York Times:* "Oxford Students Defy Ban on 'Bag Trousers,'" *New York Times,* Feb. 15, 1927, p. 1.

    "jazz attire": "Fashion's Edicts Ban 'Jazz' Attire for Men," p. 27.

    "tyranny of starch": Allen, "Vestments of the Male," p. 212; Dr. Donald A. Laird, "What Is Wrong with Men's Clothes?" cited in "Research Backs Male Revolt against Suffocation," *Literary Digest,* Aug. 17, 1929, p. 28.

    "senseless garb": "Man's Senseless Garb," *Literary Digest,* June 24, 1922, p. 21.

    "hampered the blood-stream": "Research Backs Male Revolt," p. 30; "Man's Senseless Garb," pp. 21–22; "Health in Fewer Clothes," *New York Times,* Sept. 6, 1925, sec. 2, p. 13; "Mere Man Has No Defense," *New York Times,* Oct. 29, 1925, p. 24.

    "heat stasis": "Research Backs Male Revolt," p. 28.

    A German scientist: "And the Fact Is That She's Right," *New York Times,* Oct. 29, 1925, p. 24.

    "Men are still wearing": Quoted in "Research Backs Male Revolt," p. 28.

    "When we inspect": Quoted in "Research Backs Male Revolt," p. 30. Another observer put it even more bluntly: "It is a well-known fact that a girl in an evening gown can dance a man in a dress suit to death" ("Man's Senseless Garb," p. 22).

88. "lightly and airily": "Clothes and the Man," *Hygeia*, Jan. 1929, p. 61; "Man Advised to Wear Much Less Clothing," *New York Times*, Sept. 13, 1925, sec. 9, p. 6; "Man's Senseless Garb," p. 22.

89. "gospel of lighter clothing": "On the Contrary," *Outlook*, Aug. 14, 1929, p. 617.

"dreamed of being": Ibid.

According to a 1920s survey: "The Hard-Boiled Collars of Palm Beach," *Literary Digest*, May 5, 1923, pp. 56–59, especially p. 56.

"The whole issue": "Hard-Boiled Collars," p. 56.

90. "A parade": Allen, "Vestments of the Male," p. 208.

"gather the courage": "Red Revolution in Men's Clothing," *Literary Digest*, July 3, 1937, p. 32.

"ice-cream-colored": "Colors for Men—As Told to Arthur Van Vlissingen, Jr.," *Saturday Evening Post*, Nov. 21, 1931, p. 14.

"little trio": Allen, "Vestments of the Male," p. 215.

"Plumage": "Plumage for Men," *New York Times*, Feb. 26, 1930, p. 24.

"Through the medium": Paul Nystrom, *Economics of Fashion* (New York, 1928), p. 345.

91. Those whose preference: "Plumage for Men," p. 24; "Solomon's Sartorial Glory Rivaled by Modern He-Man," *Literary Digest*, Mar. 3, 1923, p. 56; "Colors for Men," p. 14.

return to the old ways: "Want Well-Groomed Men," *New York Times*, Mar. 23, 1924, sec. 2, p. 14.

"male urge to color": "Colors for Men," p. 15.

92. "proudly patterned": Allen, "Vestments of the Male," p. 208; "Solomon's Sartorial Glory," p. 56.

"Ever since I can remember": "Colors for Men," pp. 14, 98.

93. "Many a middle-aged man": "Colors for Men," p. 98.

"world's most henpecked race": "Plumage for Men," p. 24.

"ventilated": Hawes, *Men Can Take It*, p. 137.

"porosity clothes": Twyeffort, cited in Hawes, *Men Can Take It*, pp. 136–38.

Etiquette writers: Dorothy Stote, *Men Too Wear Clothes* (New York, 1939), pp. 88, 111, 91.

95. "manuals of politeness": See, for example, Henry Lunette, *The*

American Gentleman's Guide to Politeness and Fashion (Philadelphia, 1866); Cecil B. Hartley, The Gentleman's Book of Etiquette and Manual of Politeness (Boston, 1873); John H. Young, Our Deportment, or The Manners, Conduct and Dress of the Most Refined Society (New York, 1885); Charles Harcourt, Good Form for Men: A Guide to Conduct and Dress on All Occasions (Philadelphia, 1905), p. 44.

95.   "the best jewel": Hartley, Gentleman's Book of Etiquette, p. 138.

96.   "a man may go": Hallie E. Rives, The Complete Book of Etiquette—With Social Forms for All Ages and Occasions (New York, 1926), p. 133; Ulysses Grant Dietz, "Producing What America Wanted: Jewelry from Newark's Workshops," The Glitter & the Gold: Fashioning America's Jewelry (Newark, 1997), pp. 51–65.

"presented themselves": "Colors for Men," p. 14.

"no lack": Muriel MacFarlane, "Appropriate Jewelry Never More Important," National Jeweler, Sept. 1925, p. 65; "Good Gifts for Men," National Jeweler, Dec. 1930, p. 30.

"masculine perquisite": "Military Jewelry," Jewelry Fashions: An Authoritative Style Book, Bureau of Jewelry Fashions (New York, 1917), p. 13.

"as important as": National Jeweler, Apr. 1925, p. 21.

97.   "distinctly masculine": Vogue, May 15, 1914, p. 120; June 15, 1914, p. 74.

"Any man, every man": Vogue, Dec. 15, 1910, p. 87.

"approved by Dame Fashion": Vogue, Mar. 15, 1915, p. 116.

"jewelry password": Vogue, Feb. 1, 1916, p. 118.

"Whatever the tempting glow": Rives, Complete Book of Etiquette, p. 134.

"Nothing is more vulgar": Emily Post, Etiquette (New York, 1940), p. 730.

99.   "snarl" their ties: Stote, Men Too Wear Clothes, p. 116.

"It isn't only women": Stote, Men Too Wear Clothes, p. xviii.

CHAPTER FOUR: WHERE DID YOU GET THAT HAT?

101. "something to tip": Dorothy Stote, Men Too Wear Clothes (New York, 1939), p. 1.

101. "But his hat": "Human Nature in a Hat Store: Curious Facts and Sto-
     ries about Hats and Heads, Men's Tastes and the Shapes and Colors
     of Headgear as Told by Gordon A. O'Neill, Hat Buyer for 'The
     Man's Shop,' Lord and Taylor's Department Store—New York
     City—As Reported by Merle Crowell," *American Magazine*, Mar.
     1923, p. 43.

     "As every woman knows": "$200,000,000 Worth of Hats," *Fortune*,
     Jan. 1935, p. 50.

102. "blithesome effect": "April . . . Easter . . . A New Hat!" *Ladies'
     Home Journal*, Apr. 1933, p. 3.

     "Fewer than five": "Crowns for All Occasions," *New York Times*,
     Mar. 1, 1929, p. 24.

     "swank of a Rajah": "Knox the Hatter," *American Hebrew*, May 29,
     1925, p. 114.

     "true headgear": "The Stiff Felt Hat," *New York Times*, Sept. 13,
     1914, sec. 2, p. 14.

103. "laugh at everything": "The Psychology of the Derby," *Literary
     Digest*, Apr. 6, 1929, p. 16.

     "Any man who is trim": "Human Nature in a Hat Store," p. 43.

     "closes off": "An Enemy of the Stiff Hat," *New York Times*, Sept.
     16, 1914, p. 10; "Soft Hats vs. Derbies," *New York Times*, Sept. 15,
     1914, p. 10.

     "no work of art": "Psychology of the Derby," p. 16.

     "I wish someone": "His Clothes—as Seen by Her: The Candid
     Opinions of Some Half a Hundred Young Women on the
     Momentous Subject of Male Attire," *Good Housekeeping*, July
     1909, p. 18.

     "Sometimes a man": "$200,000,000 Worth of Hats," p. 50.

105. For those who suffered: "Knox the Hatter," p. 114; "San Francisco
     Discovers a Taste for Straws," *American Hatter*, Aug. 1920, p. 106.
     Actually, panamas were misnamed. Made in Ecuador, Peru, and
     Colombia, they were merely shipped from Panama. In Latin Amer-
     ica, they were known as *jipijapas*. See "The Traffic in Panama
     Hats," *Pan-American Union Bulletin, Bulletin of the International
     Bureau of the American Republics*, Sept. 1908, pp. 483–94, especially

pp. 483ff. See also "Panama Hats," *Scientific American*, Sept. 29, 1900, p. 198.

105. "as standardized": "Hat Wearing Customs in the U.S.A.," *Notes and Queries*, Apr. 2, 1927, p. 247; "Memorabilia," *Notes and Queries*, Jan. 15, 1927, p. 38.

"Straw hats as stiff": Arthur Miller, "Before Air-Conditioning," *New Yorker*, June 22 & 29, 1998, p. 147.

"straw hat time": "And Here's Another One!" *American Hatter*, July 1921, p. 87.

"Before the 15th of May": "The Window in May," *American Hatter*, May 1910, p. 57; "And Here's Another One!" p. 87.

"The ides of March": "Good-bye to the Straw Hat," *New York Times Magazine*, Sept. 13, 1925, p. 20.

106. "may even be a Bolshevik": Ibid.

"unremarked and unmolested": Letter to the Editor from "Last Straw," *New York Times*, Sept. 22, 1925, p. 24.

"small boy": "Straw Hat's Rigid Conventions," *New York Times*, June 21, 1925, sec. 4, p. 20. "Green ties or tan shoes draw no such blows," explained one student of American sartorial conventions. "Tan shoes in Winter were once frowned on and now are common. A green or red tie stirs strong emotions because of its color, not because it is a tie. The straw hat's effects spring from within."

Nearly a quarter of a century: What follows is drawn from "Hat Wearing Customs in the U.S.A.," *Notes and Queries*, Apr. 16, 1927, p. 281.

107. "pariah company": "Memorabilia," p. 38.

"In the presence": "Hat Wearing Customs in the U.S.A.," Apr. 16, 1927, p. 281.

The gentleman also took off: "Man Needs Five Hats, Not Twelve, Hatters Reply to Tailors," *New York Times*, Feb. 28, 1929, p. 27; "Hat Wearing Customs in the U.S.A.," Apr. 16, 1927, p. 281.

"useful European": Lee M. Friedman, "Mrs. Child's Visit to a New York Synagogue in 1841," *Publications of the American Jewish Historical Society* 38 (1948–49), p. 178.

108. "feature of uniqueness": Samuel Krauss, "The Jewish Rite of Cov-

ering the Head," *Hebrew Union College Annual* 19 (1945–46), p. 123. See also "Bareheadedness," *Jewish Encyclopedia* (New York, 1902), pp. 530–33.

108. enormous psychological importance: Krauss, "Jewish Rite," p. 123. See also R. Brasch, "Why Jews Cover the Head: A Case Study in Tradition," *Commentary,* Jan. 1954, pp. 37–40.

"In our time": "Responsum 2: Propriety of Using Discarded Practices in Reform Services," *Year Book, Central Conference of American Rabbis* 65 (1955), pp. 89–90.

"act of willful": "Responsum 2," p. 90.

109. "abomination ne plus ultra": Krauss, "Jewish Rite," p. 122.

sartorially charged moment: Ruth Gay, *Unfinished People* (New York, 1996), pp. 107–08.

111. "humbly compelled": "Things—Called Women's Hats," *Hebrew Standard,* Oct. 8, 1909, p. 10.

"their decorative ideas": "The Woman and the Hat," *Independent,* Apr. 20, 1905, p. 911.

"kindling sensation": Ibid.

"much of the smartness": Mary Brooks Picken, *The Secrets of Distinctive Dress* (Scranton, 1918), p. 66.

"wield a hand mirror": "En Profile," *American Jewess,* Oct. 1895, p. 60.

112. "A hat may be": Ibid.

"any complaint": "Consider the Hat," *Ladies' Home Journal,* Oct. 1925, p. 89.

"If a woman must": Ibid.

"standardized smart hat": Ibid.

113. "as sure to have smartness": "$200,000,000 Worth of Hats," p. 54.

"When they tilt": Ibid.

"life-or-death interest": "Woman and the Hat," p. 912; "Women's Hats like Food," *New York Times,* June 27, 1920, sec. 9, p. 14.

"so much prettier": "Notes Taken in Church," *New York Times,* July 24, 1892, p. 13.

"personal preference": "A Successful Church Choir Hat," *Illustrated Milliner,* Jan. 1900, p. 33.

113.   "Pyramids of grapes": Eleanor Engels, "Put On Your Old Gay Bonnet," *Ave Maria*, Sept. 23, 1950, p. 398.

114.   Hats also enlivened: Lena Williams, "In Defense of the Church Hat," *New York Times*, May 12, 1996, city sec., p. 11. See also Bernadette Grier, Letter to the Editor, *New York Times*, city sec., June 16, 1996.

       "day of dress": Shane White and Graham White, *Stylin': African American Expressive Culture from Its Beginnings to the Zoot Suit* (Ithaca, 1998), p. 174.

       "Work clothes" : White and White, *Stylin'*, p. 176.

116.   "wearing a hat": Williams, "In Defense of the Church Hat."

       "God is awfully busy": Ibid.

       "Does Broadway": Quoted in "Keeping in Style," *Portal to America: The Lower East Side, 1870–1925*, ed. Allon Schoener (New York, 1967), p. 121.

       "unhealthy, unlovely": "The Wig—Then and Now," *Froyen Velt*, Nov. 1913, p. 1; Hutchins Hapgood, *The Spirit of the Ghetto* (New York, 1902), p. 73. See also Barbara Schreier, ed., *Becoming American Women: Clothing and the Jewish Immigrant Experience, 1880–1920* (Chicago, 1994), pp. 56–57.

       "Most Jews": Jonathan Sarna, ed., *People Walk on Their Heads* by Moses Weinberger (New York, 1982), p. 80.

118.   "The girl whose Russian": "Keeping in Style," p. 122.

       "eye-smiting display": "Easter Sunday Finds the Past in Shadow at Modern Parade," *New York Times*, Apr. 1, 1929, p. 3.

       "Prepare for Easter!": "Prepare for Easter!" *Illustrated Milliner*, Mar. 1900, editorial page; Jan. 1900, p. 3.

119.   "To do honor": "Easter Sunday in Chicago," *Illustrated Milliner*, Apr. 1910, p. 63.

       "matchless exhibition": "On the Easter Hats," *Illustrated Milliner*, May 1900, p. 51.

       "To see and be seen": "Easter Sunday at Atlantic City," *Illustrated Milliner*, May 1909, p. 13.

       "easy to greet": "The Fourteen Smartest Hats from Paris to Solve Your Easter Problem," *Ladies' Home Journal*, Apr. 1924, p. 55.

119.   "*This* is the time": Advertisement for Outlet Millinery Co., *Connecticut Hebrew Record*, Sept. 10, 1920, p. 14.

121.   "The Reason Why": *Illustrated Milliner*, Mar. 1900, p. 49.

"scandals in female modesty": Quoted in Suzy Menkes, "What's in a Hat?" *New York Times*, Feb. 27, 1994, sec. 9, p. 4.

"You can tell": Quoted in Lilly Daché, "Women's Hats—Or Are They?" *Catholic Digest*, Nov. 1946, p. 85.

"dangerous pins": "The Spring Hats," *New York Times*, May 28, 1910, p. 8; "Flowers the Rage," *Illustrated Milliner*, Feb. 1910, p. 59.

"but never has the subject": "Women's Hats Off in Church," *New York Times*, Mar. 27, 1909, p. 4. Emphasis mine.

122.   "Fancy that": "The Hats of Women," *New York Times*, Mar. 28, 1909, p. 12.

"Besides showing": "Priest Condemns Big Hats," *New York Times*, Apr. 26, 1910, p. 7.

"fancy millinery": Ibid.; "Easter Hats Not for Church," *New York Times*, Apr. 11, 1909, p. 1.

123.   "length and depth": Henry Murray Calvert, Letter to the Editor, *New York Times*, May 23, 1910, p. 6.

In one instance: "Big Hats Hide Church Fire," *New York Times*, Apr. 20, 1908, p. 1.

124.   "Pews which have": "Church Ban on Big Hats," *New York Times*, Apr. 20, 1908, p. 1.

"women to spend": "Hats of Women," p. 12; "Church Orders Hats Off," *New York Times*, Mar. 13, 1909, p. 1; "Easter Hats Not for Church," p. 1.

"These days": Henry Murray Calvert, Letter to the Editor, p. 6.

125.   "answer for more": "Church Ban on Big Hats," p. 1.

"occupies the space": "Spring Hats," p. 8.

"fad of the hour": "Captivating Hatpins," *Illustrated Milliner*, Dec. 1909, p. 82.

"Possibly to keep pace": Ibid.

"Ladies": J. H. H., Letter to the Editor, *New York Times*, Dec. 11, 1909, p. 10.

"hat evil": "Women's Hats Off in Church," p. 4.

125. "the rise of the curtain": "Hats!" *Bird-Lore,* Jan.-Feb. 1901, p. 41.

"There is no need": "Tiara—Favorite among Coiffure Ornaments," *Illustrated Milliner,* Sept. 1910, p. 93.

126. "avec chapeaux": "Hats and Things," *New York Times,* May 3, 1910, p. 12.

"Women who wear": "Safety Measure for the New Hats," *New York Times,* Apr. 13, 1908, p. 7.

"obnoxious alike": "Criticism from an Expert," *New York Times,* Apr. 8, 1909, p. 10.

"Big hats are a nuisance": Abby Hedge Coryett, Letter to the Editor, *New York Times,* June 13, 1910, p. 6.

"There is nothing": "No More Rivalry between the Large and the Small Hat; Both Equally Favored," *Illustrated Milliner,* Oct. 1911, p. 23.

127. "floral and faunal marvel": "Criticism from an Expert," p. 10.

"right hat": Kay Sullivan, "Lilly Daché: Queen of Hats," *Catholic Digest,* June 1957, p. 24.

CHAPTER FIVE: OH, MY ACHING FEET!

129. "Men and women": "Make Your Feet Happy," advertisement for Holeproof Hosiery, n.d., Courtesy Peter H. Schweitzer.

"The era of Good Sense": "A Man with an Idea," *Shoe Retailer,* Oct. 1898, p. 67.

130. "shoe in all its forms": Woods Hutchinson, "Shoes and the Man," *Good Housekeeping,* July 1912, p. 85.

90 percent of Americans: Elizabeth Sears, "Wanted—A Shoe!" *Ladies' Home Journal,* Dec. 1919, p. 81.

"sardines in a tin": Hutchinson, "Shoes and the Man," p. 85.

Eureka: Advertisement for Black & White Cravanette Boots, Program, Belasco Theatre, July 24, 1911; Dudley Joy Morton, "The Human Foot and the Shoe Industry," n.d., pp. 7–8, Collection of the New York Academy of Medicine.

"the most aesthetic": Helen Ecob, *The Well-Dressed Woman: A Study in the Practical Application to Dress of the Laws of Health, Art and Morals* (New York, 1892), p. 158.

132. "stand, walk and run": Charlotte C. West, "High Heels," *Ladies'*
     Home Journal, Jan. 1920, p. 121.

     "A trim foot": West, "High Heels," p. 39.

     "anything more senseless": "Abominations in Fashions," *New York*
     Times, Mar. 28, 1869, p. 4.

     "Civilized beings": West, "High Heels," p. 121.

133. Irritability:"What Bad Shoes Do," *Literary Digest,* Apr. 27, 1929,
     p. 22.

     "No woman": Sears, "Wanted," p. 81.

     "No girl": Ibid.

     "Nature planned": Ibid.

     "Americanization begins": *Shoe Retailer,* Sept. 16, 1903, p. 168.

134. "What's wrong here?": Quoted in Barbara Schreier, ed., *Becoming*
     American Women: Clothing and the Jewish Immigrant Experience,
     1880–1920 (Chicago, 1994), p. 63.

     Another new arrival: Gina M. Tarentino, "The Language of
     Clothes: Italian Immigrant Women in New York City,
     1880–1930," unpublished student paper, Gallatin Division of
     Graduate Studies, New York University, May 1995, p. 11.

135. "Nice patent-leather": Program Guide, Harlem Opera House, May
     1902, p. 5.

136. The girls, reported social worker: Sophonisba Breckenridge, *New*
     Homes for Old (New York, 1921), pp. 173–74.

138. "thumbless mittens": Hutchinson, "Shoes and the Man," pp. 87, 88.

     "many of the so-called": Hutchinson, "Shoes and the Man," p. 87.

     Industry studies confirmed: "The Female of the Species—Not as
     Deadly as the Male," *Shoe Retailer,* Aug. 14, 1920, p. 71; "How
     Women Purchase Shoes," *Journal of Home Economics,* Mar. 1938,
     p. 177.

     "altar of vanity": Hutchinson "Shoes and the Man," p. 84.

     "it is a fact": "The Feminine Foot," *New York Times,* Jan. 15, 1909, p. 8.

139. "unwilling, without mathematical demonstration": Edward Lyman
     Munson, *The Soldier's Foot and the Military Shoe: A Handbook for*
     Officers and Noncommissioned Officers of the Line (Fort Leaven-
     worth 1912), p. 78.

139. "universal aversion": W. L. Mann and S. A. Folsom, *A Manual on Foot Care and Shoe Fitting for Officers of the U.S. Navy and U.S. Marine Corps* (Philadelphia, 1920), pp. 78, 76.

"a foot soldier": "Fitting the Shoe to the Soldier: The Evolution of a Satisfactory System of Measuring the Foot," *Scientific American*, Jan. 18, 1919, p. 56; Mann and Folsom, *Manual*, p. 1. See also "Shoe-Fitting with the X-Ray," *Literary Digest*, Sept. 13, 1912, p. 418.

"fact rather than opinion": Munson, *Soldier's Foot*, p. 42.

"Shoes are properly": Munson, *Soldier's Foot*, p. 47.

141. "Can anyone": Arthur L. Evans, *Correct Shoe Fitting*, Retail Shoe Salesman's Institute, Training Course for Retail Shoe Salesmen, vol. 2 (Boston, 1920), p. 10.

"True salesmanship": George F. Hamilton, *Retail Shoe Salesmanship*, Retail Shoe Salesman's Institute, Training Course for Retail Shoe Salesmen, vol. 1 (Boston, 1920), p. v.

"Races differ": Evans, *Correct Shoe Fitting*, p. 202.

"principles of correct shoe fitting": Evans, *Correct Shoe Fitting*, p. vii.

142. "None can minimize": Evans, *Correct Shoe Fitting*, p. 7.

"Listen to any group": "This New Art of Staying Young," advertisement for Cantilever shoes, *Literary Digest*, June 16, 1928, p. 4.

"Built for service": Sears, "Wanted," p. 81.

For years, home economics instructors: The following account is drawn from "What Bad Shoes Do."

143. "Mirrors have a reputation": Quoted in "Putting American Women 'On Another Footing,'" *New York Times*, Oct. 12, 1919, sec. 8, p. 10.

"another footing": Ibid.; Sears, "Wanted," p. 81; "Y.W.C.A. Urges Shoe Reform," *New York Times*, Apr. 12, 1919, p. 14.

"We freed ourselves": Sears, "Wanted," pp. 81–82.

144. "as good to look at": What follows is drawn from "Y.W.C.A. Urges Shoe Reform"; "Shoes," *Journal of Home Economics*, Jan. 1920, p. 40. See also Sears, "Wanted," pp. 81–82.

"Style and comfort": "The Comfort Shoe That's Also *Smart*," advertisement for Modease shoes, *Shoe Retailer*, Sept. 4, 1920.

144. "anatomically perfect": "Style Plus Comfort," advertisement for Physical Culture shoes, *Shoe Retailer*, Aug. 14, 1920, p. 44.

Foot Savers: "Worthy Shoes," advertisement for J & K Foot Savers, *Ladies' Home Journal*, Oct. 1925, p. 72.

"women's philosophy": Quoted in "Putting American Women 'On Another Footing,'" p. 10.

"Good feet": Women's Foundation for Health, *A Handbook on Positive Health* (New York, 1922), p. 23. See also the chapter "Feet, Posture, Shoes and Walking," pp. 96–106.

145. "Work the toes": U.S. Public Health Service, *The Road to Health* (Washington, 1920).

"war against tight shoes": "A War against Tight Shoes," *Literary Digest*, July 15, 1922, pp. 23–24.

one shoe salesman reported in 1920: Evans, *Correct Shoe Fitting*, p. 6.

147. "start people thinking": Dudley J. Morton, Foreword, *Oh, Doctor! My Feet!* (New York, 1939).

Most people knew: Morton, *Oh, Doctor!* pp. 124, 82.

"dead sure": Elizabeth R. Duval, "Fashion's Fantasies for Feet," *New York Times Magazine*, Apr. 14, 1940, p. 8.

"event": Hamilton, *Retail Shoe Salesmanship*, p. 6.

CHAPTER SIX: THE TRUTH ABOUT FUR

149. "Fur-fur-fur": "The Winter Modes," unidentified broadside, Dec. 1919, p. 110, Courtesy Peter H. Schweitzer.

"procession of wild beasts": Minnie Maddern Fiske, "What a Deformed Thief This Fashion Is," *Ladies' Home Journal*, Sept. 1921, p. 20.

151. "fifty-five hundred dollars": Clara Belle Thompson, "Furs—Their Beauty and Their Artifice," *Ladies' Home Journal*, Nov. 1925, p. 73.

"become universal": "Furs without Traps," *New York Times*, Dec. 1, 1924, p. 16.

"noisy, hey-hey college boy": Jonathan B. Bingham, "Current Affairs and Raccoon Coats," *Vital Speeches of the Day*, Mar. 25, 1935, p. 403; "Your Fur Coat at Home," *Collier's*, Feb. 5, 1927, p. 19.

"summer furs": Florence B. Rose, "Of Course Women Will Wear

Furs This Summer," *American Weekly Jewish News,* Apr. 26, 1918, p. 17; *Fur Age,* Dec. 1920, p. 59.

"If our grandmothers": Rose, "Of Course Women Will Wear Furs This Summer," p. 17.

"It doesn't always stay": Ibid.; "St. Louis, Furrier to the American Woman—and the World," *Literary Digest,* Apr. 10, 1920, p. 88.

152. "conferring beauty upon": Abraham Gottlieb, *Fur Truths: The Story of Fur and the Fur Business* (New York, 1927), p. 63.

What's more, furs now came: Thompson, "Furs—Their Beauty and Their Artifice," p. 72.

"Certainly the pliancy": Henri Bendel, "Fur, the Twentieth Century Extravagance: In the Entire History of Costume Its Use Was Never So General," *Arts and Decoration,* Nov. 1923, p. 44.

"style element": "St. Louis, Furrier to the American Woman," p. 88.

153. "fur for every face": Thompson, "Furs—Their Beauty and Their Artifice," p. 73.

"durable, less durable": "Furs and Their Care," *Literary Digest,* Sept. 27, 1924 p. 29; Gottlieb, *Fur Truths,* passim; Anna Bird Stewart, *The Fur Book of Knowledge* (New York, 1926), p. 93.

154. "about as common": "Campaign to Urge Less Wearing of Fur," *New York Times,* July 5, 1925, sec. 7, p. 8.

"In these days": "St. Louis, Furrier to the American Woman," p. 83.

156. "coquettish adornment": Octave Uzanne, "Story of Furs and Muffs," *Good Housekeeping,* Sept. 1912, p. 334.

"à la mode": Fiske, "What a Deformed Thief," p. 20.

"It is not for warmth": Fiske, "What a Deformed Thief," pp. 20–21.

"back into the hinterland": Lucy Furman, "The Price of Furs: A Plea for Humane Trapping," *Atlantic,* Feb. 1928, p. 206.

157. "seen only in museums": "Call Milady's Furs Peril to Wildlife," *New York Times,* May 19, 1922, p. 19.

"elaborate neckpieces": "Campaign to Urge Less Wearing of Furs," p. 8. See also "Fourth Blue Cross 'Crusade' Levelled at Open Season," *Fur Age Monthly,* Aug. 1926, p. 29.

"Curriculum of Humane Education": "Furs without Traps," p. 16.

"fur antis": "They Take Credit," *Fur Age Monthly,* Aug. 1926, p. 62.

158. A year later: On the origins of the Audubon Society, see Joseph Kastner, "Long before Furs, It Was Feathers That Stirred Reformist Ire," *Smithsonian*, July 1994, pp. 96–104. See also "Tragedy of the White Heron, Victim of Woman's Vanity," *New York Times*, Aug. 13, 1905, part 3, p. 4. For use of the term "bird protection," see *Bird-Lore: A Bi-Monthly Magazine Devoted to the Study and Protection of Birds. The Official Organ of the Audubon Societies*, Aug. 1899, p. 138.

"movements of the age": "Notes," *Bird-Lore*, Oct. 1900, p. 166.

"white lists": "Notes," *Bird-Lore*, Oct. 1900, p. 163; "A Good Example," *Bird-Lore*, Aug. 1901, p. 150.

"Audubonnets": "Report from the Rhode Island Society," *Bird-Lore*, Dec. 1899, p. 204; *Bird-Lore*, Aug. 1899, pp. 138–39.

"proved conclusively": "Report of the Rhode Island Society," *Bird-Lore*, Aug. 1900, p. 131.

"readjust her conscience": "Wanted—The Truth," *Bird-Lore*, Feb. 1900, p. 32.

160. "Taking plumes": William Deutcher, "The Ostrich," *National Association of Audubon Societies Educational Leaflet Number 10, Bird-Lore*, Mar.–Apr. 1905, p. 154.

"I pledge myself": *Bird-Lore*, Nov.–Dec. 1906, p. 219; "Results Achieved in 1907," *Annual Report of Audubon Societies for 1907, Bird-Lore*, Nov.–Dec. 1907, p. 299.

"making cemeteries": Letter to the Editor from "Humane," *New York Times*, Jan. 15, 1909, p. 8.

"And these are the creatures": Letter to the Editor from W. J., *New York Times*, Apr. 20, 1910, p. 8.

"destruction of birds": Alice Stone Blackwell, Letter to the Editor, *New York Times*, May 3, 1910, p. 12.

161. "To accuse women": "The Bird on a Woman's Hat," *Ladies' Home Journal*, May 1897, p. 14.

"tender-hearted": Editorial, *Harper's Bazaar*, Nov. 18, 1899, p. 974.

"really nice people": "Back to First Principles," *Bird-Lore*, Oct. 1902, p. 168.

161. Surely no lady: Mrs. G. B. Satterlee, Letter to the Editor, *New York Times*, Apr. 24, 1910, p. 12.

"real loidies": "Hats!" *Bird-Lore*, Jan.–Feb. 1901, p. 418.

162. "The foreign-born": "Aliens," *Bird-Lore*, Oct. 1905, p. 252.

"commercial interests": See, for example, "Mis-Statements vs. the Truth about Bird Protection and Fancy Feathers," *Illustrated Milliner*, June 1909, pp. 61–62.

"join in the great": "Results Achieved in 1907," p. 299.

"We must take up": "The Millinery Trade Organ," *Bird-Lore*, Apr. 1906, p. 22.

Dismissing the society as: These characterizations are cited in "Back to First Principles," p. 171; "The Audubon Society and Its New Scarecrow," *Illustrated Milliner*, June 1910, p. 51; "Mis-Statements vs. the Truth," p. 62.

163. "Who furnishes birds": Mabel Osgood Wright, "Bird Protection and Merchant Milliners," *Bird-Lore*, Aug. 1900, p. 129.

"continually [took] new form": "The Charm of Ostrich, Paradise and Aigrettes," *Illustrated Milliner*, Apr. 1911, p. 34.

"imitation aigrette": "Notes and News from Near and Far: The Audubon Aigrette," *Illustrated Milliner*, Feb. 1911, p. 153. An advertisement for the Neargrette appears in *Illustrated Milliner*, Apr. 1911, p. 102.

165. "law and the lady": "Hats!" p. 41.

"crusaders against cruelty": "Humane Traps: Crusaders against Cruelty Seek to Alleviate the Torture of Animals," *Literary Digest*, Sept. 26, 1936, p. 31.

Lucy Furman: Furman, "Price of Furs," pp. 208–09.

166. "even the horrors": "Cruelties of Fashion," *Literary Digest*, May 18, 1929, p. 30.

"should not be tolerated": *Anti-Steel-Trap League News*, Feb. 1931, p. 2.

"act of essential sinfulness": "Crusaders of Mercy," *Commonweal*, Nov. 5, 1930, p. 4; "What Are You Doing to Help?" *Anti-Steel-Trap League News*, Oct. 1932, p. 9. Emphasis mine.

167. "men engaged in humane work": *Anti-Steel-Trap League News*, Feb. 1931, p. 1.

167.   Boy Scouts: "Boy Scouts of America Busy," *Anti-Steel-Trap League News,* Feb. 1932, p. 15.

    Who Killed Brer Rabbit?: Barbara Euphan Todd, "Who Killed Brer Rabbit?" *Anti-Steel-Trap League News,* May 1931, p. 11.

168.   "Don't ask for any furs": "Christmas Furs," *Anti-Steel-Trap League News,* Dec. 1937, p. 2.

    In 1917: Maude Radford Warren, "From Trap Line to Fifth Avenue," *Saturday Evening Post,* Feb. 15, 1930, p. 97. See also "Mink on the Move," *Business Week,* Jan. 18, 1941, p. 54.

169.   "coddled almost as much": Elizabeth Frazer, "Milady's Fur Coat," *Good Housekeeping,* Aug. 1937, p. 170.

    America's "peltry": "Thriving Peltry," *Business Week,* Feb. 8, 1941, p. 20.

    "Furs give us pleasure!": Frazer, "Milady's Fur Coat," p. 25.

    "A fur coat": Ruth Glazer, "West Bronx: Food, Shelter, Clothing," *Commentary,* June 1949, p. 583.

CHAPTER SEVEN: SAY IT WITH JEWELRY

171.   "the jeweler's window": "The Vogue in Precious Jewels," *Vogue,* May 1, 1910, p. 21. Portions of this chapter originally appeared in my essay "Jewelry: The Natural Gift," in Ulysses Grant Dietz, ed., *The Glitter & the Gold: Fashioning America's Jewelry* (Newark, 1997), pp. 19–33.

    "I have not yet": Muriel MacFarlane, "Things That Are Selling and Salable," *National Jeweler & Optician,* May 1915, p. 357.

172.   "one of the few ways": Hallie E. Rives, *The Complete Book of Etiquette—With Social Forms for All Ages and Occasions* (New York, 1926), p. 131.

    "This *is* a gift-giving age": Rives, *Complete Book of Etiquette,* p. 68; Colonel John Shepard, "Gifts That Last," *National Jeweler,* Dec. 1920, p. 72.

    "philosophy": "Philosophy of Presents," *Harper's Weekly,* Nov. 19, 1910, p. 21.

    "one smart woman": "What One Smart Woman Gives Another," *Vogue,* Dec. 15, 1910, p. 47.

"gift that lasts": *National Jeweler,* Dec. 1925, p. 23.

"Why not say it": "Equalizing the Sexes," *National Jeweler,* July 1925, p. 18; *National Jeweler,* Dec. 1920, p. 14.

173. "die with the passing": *National Jeweler,* Dec. 1925, p. 23.

175. "fine jewelry capital": Dietz, *Glitter & the Gold,* p. 11.

"The fact that the purse": "The Limitless Possibilities of the Limited Purse," *Jewelry Fashions: An Authoritative Style Book,* Bureau of Jewelry Fashions (New York, 1917), p. 13.

"Santa Claus knows": *National Jeweler,* Dec. 1925, p. 23.

"interesting insect jewelry": "Some Interesting Insect Jewelry," *National Jeweler & Optician,* June 1911, p. 257; Muriel MacFarlane, "Change Adds to the Spice of Life," *National Jeweler,* May 1925, p. 67.

"As a boon": "Old Favorites in New Guises," *Jewelry Fashions,* p. 44.

"substantial quality": *Vogue,* June 14, 1914, p. 74; *National Jeweler,* Apr. 1925, p. 21.

"dainty articles": "Where Lady Clerks Excel," *National Jeweler,* May 1920, p. 84.

"A gift at Easter": *National Jeweler,* Apr. 1925, p. 7.

"Thousands are being sold": "Rosary and Locket," *National Jeweler,* Apr. 1920, p. 93.

176. "Whether she is three": "Every Woman Has a Birthday," *National Jeweler,* Apr. 1925, p. 33.

"privilege of wearing": "Birthdays and the 21st in Particular," *Jewelry Fashions,* p. 24.

"purely spontaneous": Emily Post, *Etiquette: The Blue Book of Social Usage,* new and enlarged ed. (New York, 1927), p. 301; Rives, *Complete Book of Etiquette,* p. 68; "The Wedding Question and Its Several Answers," *Jewelry Fashions,* p. 14.

"outward and visible sign": Mrs. Burton Kingsland, "Good Manners and Good Form," *Ladies' Home Journal,* Mar. 1909, p. 44.

177. "even the most impulsive girl": Maude C. Cooke, *Social Life, or The Manners and Customs of Polite Society* (Philadelphia, 1896), p. 160; Rives, *Complete Book of Etiquette,* p. 64.

"Fashion," it was said: Post, *Etiquette,* p. 302.

Against a steady drumbeat: See, for example, "Too Much Jewelry Worn in Foreign Society," *Vogue*, Nov. 1896, p. 406; Rives, *Complete Book of Etiquette*, pp. 134–39; "Limitless Possibilities of the Limited Purse," p. 13; Walter B. Houghton, *American Etiquette and the Rules of Politeness* (New York, 1883), p. 257.

177. "It has always been": Post, *Etiquette*, p. 583.

178. "We find things": Thorstein Veblen, *The Theory of the Leisure Class* (1899; New York, 1994), pp. 169, 124.

"We have gone": Edward Bok, "A Woman's Questions," *Ladies' Home Journal*, Apr. 1905, p. 16; Helen Watterson Moody, "The American Woman and Dress," *Ladies' Home Journal*, June 1901, p. 15.

"Santa Claus in the Pulpit": Washington Gladden, "Santa Claus in the Pulpit," *Santa Claus on a Lark* (New York, 1890), pp. 163–69.

179. "Good taste is simplicity": "Good Taste in Clothes for Girls—A Chat by Mrs. Ralston," *Ladies' Home Journal*, May 1910, p. 93.

"He may not know much": "What I Did with My Two Daughters," *Ladies' Home Journal*, Mar. 1908, p. 56.

"getting beauty into the classroom": Mary Polson, "Color Reaction of School Children," *Journal of Home Economics*, June 1926, p. 301.

180. "overdress": Mrs. M. F. Armstrong, *Habits and Manners, Revised Edition. Adapted to General Use* (Hampton, 1888), pp. 17, 77, 26, 29.

"love jewels more": "Suit Your Ornaments to Your Style," *American Jewess*, July 1899, p. 45.

"The love for gems": Ibid. See also Jenna Weissman Joselit, "Mirror, Mirror on the Wall: Clothing, Identity, and the Modern Jewish Experience," in Deborah Dash Moore and Ilan S. Troen, eds., *Divergent Centers* (forthcoming, Yale University Press), for more on "Jewish ostentation."

"Hebrew women are often": Countess Annie de Montague, "Love of Jewels Justified," *American Jewess*, Sept. 1897, pp. 262–64.

181. Rosa Sonneschein: Jack Nusan Porter, "Rosa Sonneschein and the *American Jewess* Revisited: New Historical Information on an Early American Zionist and Jewish Feminist," *American Jewish*

Archives, Nov. 1980, p. 129. On the *American Jewess* itself, see the entry in *Jewish Women in America: An Historical Encyclopedia,* ed. Paula E. Hyman and Deborah Dash Moore (New York, 1998), pp. 39–42.

181. "rather showy": "Suit Your Ornaments," p. 45.

"spell of Eastern fancies": Emil G. Hirsch, "The Modern Jewess," *American Jewess,* Apr. 1895, p. 10.

"ruling traits": Gustav Gottheil, "The Jewess as She Was and Is," *Ladies' Home Journal,* Dec. 1897, p. 21.

"Under the banner": Rosa Sonneschein, "The American Jewess," *American Jewess,* Feb. 1898, p. 209.

"as readily as": Ibid.

182. "sacrificed at the shrine": Hirsch, "Modern Jewess," p. 11.

183. "more like violets": "What Our Girls Can Do," *Sabbath School Companion of Kahal Kadosh Beth Elohim,* Charleston, S.C., Jan. 1895, p. 7.

"conquer [their] innate desire": "The Jewess at Summer Resorts," *American Jewess,* June 1895, pp. 139–40; "Missionaries Wanted," *American Jewess,* May 1899, p. 46; "Go On Conquering," *American Jewess,* Jan. 1899, p. 45.

"There is not the slightest": "Jewels No Longer Synonymous with Jewess," *American Jewess,* Jan. 1899, pp. 44–45.

"shrieking": Fannie Hurst, quoted in an interview by Marion Golde, "The Modern Ghetto Girl: Does She Lack Refinement?" *American Weekly Jewish News,* Mar. 22, 1918, p. 11.

The immigrant Jewish girl: I would like to thank Riv-Ellen Prell for bringing this material to my attention.

184. "restraining force": Hurst, quoted in Golde, "Modern Ghetto Girl," p. 11.

"veritable jewelry store": Abraham Cahan, *The Rise of David Levinsky* (1917; New York, 1960), p. 367.

Invited guests included: What follows is drawn from Marion Golde, "The Modern Ghetto Girl: Does She Lack Refinement? Discussed by Fannie Hurst and Sophie Irene Loeb," *American Weekly Jewish News,* Mar. 22, 1918, p. 11; Golde, "The Modern Ghetto

Girl: Does She Lack Refinement? Discussed by Mrs. Asch, Mme. Nazimova and Mr. Foshko," *American Weekly Jewish News*, Mar. 29, 1918, pp. 10–11; Miriam Shomer Zunser, "The 'Ghetto Girl' Once Again," *American Weekly Jewish News*, Apr. 19, 1918, p. 15.

184. "hopelessly vulgar": Golde, "Modern Ghetto Girl," Mar. 29, 1918, p. 10.

185. "imposition of circumstance": Nazimova, quoted in "Modern Ghetto Girl," Mar. 29, 1918, p. 11.

clothing that "glared": Foshko, quoted in "Modern Ghetto Girl," Mar. 29, 1918, p. 10.

"This crudity will pass": Asch, quoted in "Modern Ghetto Girl," Mar. 29, 1918, p. 10.

186. "laws which govern": Post, *Etiquette*, 1936 ed., p. 721.

Emily Post tended to agree: Post, *Etiquette*, 1936 ed., pp. 682–85, especially pp. 684–85.

CONCLUSION: EMPHATICALLY MODERN

189. "strange, but provocative": "Scolding Show," *Time*, Dec. 11, 1944, p. 50.

"You can't tell them apart": "The Unfashionable Body," *New Yorker*, Dec. 9, 1944, p. 24; "Scolding Show"; "The Case against Clothes," *Newsweek*, Dec. 11, 1944, p. 102.

"Dame Fashion": *Kingston Leader*, Dec. 11, 1944, n.p., in *Are Clothes Modern?* Museum of Modern Art Scrapbook, 1944, Archives of the Museum of Modern Art, New York.

"expert on the superfluousness": Edward Alden Jewell, "Art: So Many Things," *New York Times*, Dec. 3, 1944, sec. 2, p. 8.

190. "violently popular": Janet H. O'Connell, Supervisor of Circulating Exhibitions, to Donald C. Vaughan of Brooks Brothers, New York, May 3, 1945, Museum of Modern Art Public Information Scrapbooks, MF16; 246, Archives of the Museum of Modern Art.

"uneconomical": "Unfashionable Body," p. 24.

"emphatically" modern: " 'Are Clothes Modern?' Asks the Modern Museum. 'Emphatically Yes,' Says *Vogue*," *Vogue*, Feb. 1, 1945, p. 121.

190.　"Girls will be boys": Jane Cobb, "Girls Will Be Boys," *New York Times Magazine*, Nov. 3, 1940, p. 10.

By then, women clad: Virginia Pope, "Fashions for War Workers," *New York Times Magazine*, Oct. 4, 1942, pp. 28–29.

191.　"slacks": Elizabeth F. Valentine, "Slacks: A Woman Takes Over Another Masculine Garment," *New York Times Magazine*, Mar. 1, 1942, pp. 16–17; "War-Time Living: Pants," *Time*, Apr. 13, 1942, p. 19.

"zooming all the time": "War-Time Living," p. 18.

"Slacks look wonderfully well": "A Primer on Pants," *Vogue*, Apr. 1, 1942, pp. 74–75.

"generational phenomenon": Social Research, Inc., *Chicagoland Women and Their Clothing: A Motivational Research Prepared for the Chicago Tribune* (Chicago, 1957), pp. 22, 21.

"whether living in the heart": *Chicagoland Women and Their Clothing*, pp. 19, 21.

"Get casual, man!": "Get Casual, Man!" *Newsweek*, July 20, 1953, p. 76.

192.　"marriage of Orlon and Dacron": "In-Town Buyers," *New Yorker*, Jan. 26, 1952, p. 19.

"precisely two inches": "Shorts," *New Yorker*, July 31, 1954, p. 11.

"Giving a leg up": Ibid.

192.　"alarmed over the male tendency": "Confident Feeling: Formal Wear Institute," *New Yorker*, May 5, 1951, p. 26, 25.

"declaration of independence": Fritz Redl, "Zoot Suits: An Interpretation," *Survey*, Oct. 1943, p. 260.

"I thought it was as crazy": What follows is drawn from Meyer Berger, "Zoot Suit Originated in Georgia," *New York Times*, June 11, 1943, p. 21. See also Stuart Cosgrove, "The Zoot-Suit and Style Warfare," *History Workshop Journal* 18 (Autumn 1984), pp. 77–91.

193.　"Behold, the bar mitzvah": Benjamin Kreitman and Joyce Kreitman, "Fashions for the Synagogue," *United Synagogue Review*, Spring 1972, p. 31.

"the unusual thing": "Answers to Questions: Head Covering for

Women in Church," *Homiletic and Pastoral Review,* Dec. 1946, p. 218.

193. "wisp of a veil": Joe Breig, "Should Women Wear (Ugh) Hats in Church?" *Ave Maria,* Aug. 18, 1962, p. 19.

the yarmulke was for men: Kreitman and Kreitman, "Fashions for the Synagogue," p. 15.

"Is there any basis": "Answers to Questions," p. 218.

194. "Our children are seeking": Hillel Silverman, "New Directions for the Synagogue and the Rabbinate," *United Synagogue Review,* Fall 1972, p. 8.

Some Catholic priests: See, for example, "Questions Answered," *Homiletic and Pastoral Review,* Jan. 1951, p. 374; "Questions and Answers: Discarding Clerical Dress," *Clergy Review,* July 1950, pp. 47–49.

"Marilyke tag": "The Marilyke Look," *Time,* June 27, 1955, p. 64.

195. "lookalikeness": Grace Glueck, "Now His *Is* Hers," *New York Times Magazine,* Sept. 20, 1964, p. 45.

"Morality is individual": Cynthia Lindsay, "Whither the Bra," *McCall's,* Nov. 1969, p. 138.

Illustration Credits

Grateful acknowledgment is made to the following individuals and institutions for permission to publish material from their collections: Miriam Jick Cohen, Bellerose, New York; Peter H. Schweitzer, New York; the Adirondack Museum, Blue Mountain Lake, New York; Hadassah, the Women's Zionist Organization of America, Inc. ; the National Museum of American Jewish History, Philadelphia; the Newark Museum, New Jersey; the Research Libraries of the New York Public Library; the Estate of Richard

Samuel Roberts; and the Tamiment Library, New York University.

This material appears on the following pages:

The Adirondack Museum: 24.

Miriam Jick Cohen: 117.

Hadassah, the Women's Zionist Organization of America, Inc.: 17, 26, 29, 118.

Jenna Weissman Joselit: 49, 50, 61, 78, 88, 98, 127, 132, 142, 143, 146, 156, 166, 187.

The New York Public Library, Humanities and Social Sciences Library: 52, 54, 95, 100, 123, 140, 159, 164.

The New York Public Library, The Performing Arts Research Collections: 45.

The New York Public Library, Schomburg Center for Research in Black Culture: 114.

The New York Public Library, Science, Industry and Business Library: 131, 137, 141, 152, 153, 154.

The National Museum of American Jewish History: 176.

The Newark Museum: 174.

The Estate of Richard Samuel Roberts: 115.

Peter H. Schweitzer: 9, 10, 11, 13, 18, 21, 36, 38, 42, 47, 48, 56, 57, 58, 59, 72, 74, 77, 79, 81, 82, 84, 86, 90, 91, 92, 93, 94, 102, 103, 104, 106, 109, 110, 112, 120, 128, 133, 134, 135, 136, 148, 150, 155, 168, 170, 173, 175, 177, 182.

The Tamiment Library, New York University: 6.

Acknowledgments

"How eloquent clothes are when they run in and out of the mind," observed writer Nathalie S. Colby in 1925. But "marshalling them into the trim square of a printed column is another matter." I know exactly what she means. Where paintings and personalities, historical events and eyewitness accounts lend themselves to words, clothes tend to resist. The writerly imagination alone is not always enough to bring them to life. Fortunately, I've been able to avail myself of a community of people who not only shared my interest in clothing and stimulated my thinking but made it possible for me to spend a number of years, happily, doing little else.

The generous financial support of the Lucius N. Littauer Foundation and the encouragement of its program director,

Pamela Ween Brumberg, were invaluable, as was a fellowship at the University of Pennsylvania's Center for Advanced Judaic Studies.

Archivists and librarians, those unsung heroes of the historical enterprise, enabled me to consult a wide range of materials, from advertisements and broadsides to sermons and zoot suits. For their efforts on my behalf, I would especially like to thank Y. O. Alleyne, formerly of the Microfilms Division of the New York Public Library; Kenneth Cobb, director of the New York City Municipal Archives; Jerold Pepper, director of the Library of the Adirondack Museum in Blue Mountain Lake, New York; Judith Leifer of Penn's Center for Advanced Judaic Studies; Noel McFerrin of St. Charles' Seminary, in Philadelphia; Julie Miller, formerly of the Ratner Center Archives for the Study of Conservative Judaism at the Jewish Theological Seminary of America; Patti Ponzoli of the Interlibrary Loan Office at Princeton University; and Susan Woodland of the Hadassah Archives.

My students at the Jewish Theological Seminary, New York University, and Princeton University sharpened my perspective on the sartorial, as did conversations with Lorraine Fuhrmann, Jane Przybysz, Dale Rosengarten, Jeffrey Shandler, and Viviana Zelizer, each of whom alerted me to the existence of material I might otherwise have missed. Milliner Jeffrey Moss graciously shared with me the details of his own research into the life of Lilly Daché. Peter H. Schweitzer's unflagging enthusiasm for America's material culture fired my own as well as furnished most of the visual delights that enliven these pages.

Still, were it not for Sara Bershtel, my beloved editor, this book would have remained an inert assemblage of words. Thanks to her gentle ways and her fierce, uncompromising intellect, *A Perfect Fit* was coaxed into being. Riva Hocherman's encouragement, Roslyn Schloss's deft and sensitive copyediting, Fritz Metsch's artistry, and Shara Kay's cheerful involvement with a seemingly endless stream of details added to, and enhanced, the process of book-making.

Through it all, as stacks of index cards and piles of photocopies grew and grew, taking up what appeared to be permanent residence in our home, my husband, Joz, bore his lot cheerfully. His unwavering support, coupled with his own love of both books and clothes, enabled me to write under the most propitious of circumstances.

A Perfect Fit is dedicated to the memory of my grandmother Rochel Leah, or Lily, as she was called in this country. As I was growing up, my mother, Alice Snyder Weissman, never seemed to tire of telling my siblings and me of our grandmother's keen eye, nimble fingers, and acute fashion sense, hoping, perhaps, that we might emulate her. Alas, we didn't. All the same, I'd like to think that in writing about Americans and their clothing I've inherited, and passed on, a bit of my grandmother's pleasure in making something for someone else.

Index

Weinstein, Emanuel, 192
Wesley, John, 121
West, Charlotte C., 132
Well-Dressed Woman, The (Ecob),
    49–50
"wheelwomen," 55
White, Graham, 114–16
White, Shane, 114–16
Willard, Frances, 46, 51
Williams, Fannie Barrier, 37, 39
Wise, Stephen S., 65–66
Wm. Henne & Company, 144
womanliness, 5
    ideal of, 58, 97
    multiple notions of, 89
    prettiness in, 43, 44, 59
    religious leaders' vision of, 65
    short skirt and, 61–63
    variations on theme of, 73
women
    in anti-trapping campaign,
        167–68
    and bird protection, 160–61
    emancipation of, 72
    hats, 101–2, 110*f*, 111–27
    and jewelry, 95, 171–72
    as latter-day muses, 45*f*
    pledge for, 41
    professionalization of skills of, 16
    responsibility in fur trade, 156–57
    and secondhand clothes, 19–20
    shoes, 132–38, 142–47

slaves to fashion, 32–33
    see also African American women;
        farm women; immigrant
        women; Jewish immigrant
        women; working women;
        younger women
women's associations
    making clothes for less fortunate,
        15–16
Woods, E. M., 82–83
working women, 23, 35, 73
    furs, 151
    jewelry for, 35
    and sensible dress, 53–55
    shoes, 133
    skirt length, 60
World War II, 169, 190–91
wristwatch, 35, 96–97, 98*f*, 175

X rays, 139, 142–43

yarmulke, 108, 111, 193
Yezierska, Anzia, 2
younger women
    and corsets, 60
    and sensible dress, 53–55
    and skirt length, 62
YWCA
    Department of Social Hygiene,
        143–46

zoot suit, 192–93

ABOUT THE AUTHOR

JENNA WEISSMAN JOSELIT is currently a visiting professor of American Studies at Princeton University and the author of numerous works of cultural history, including *The Wonders of America: Reinventing Jewish Culture 1880–1950* (winner of the National Jewish Book Award in History). Joselit has also curated and consulted on more than thirty exhibitions throughout the country. She lives in New York City.